CW01651332

Building Churches with Apostles and Prophets

Colin Cooper, Sierd de Jong, Dick Iverson, Chip Kawalsingh
Memos Sakellariou, Gordon Tose, Anthony Tselentakis

Ministers Fellowship Global
www.ministersfellowshipglobal.com

About the Authors

Colin Cooper

Colin became a Christian at the age of 18 and was ordained a Pastor in the Assemblies of God in his 30s. He was part of the Home Missions Team planting churches in un-reached areas of Britain and now lives in Huddersfield where he is an elder at Huddersfield Christian Fellowship after handing over the Pastorate to Jonny & Wendy Skinner. He is married to Sue, has two children and eight grandchildren.

Colin is the leader of MFG (Ministers Fellowship Global).

As well as having a heart for Europe, he also travels extensively in Africa, India and the USA. He has a heart to see lives changed by the power of the Holy Spirit and people growing in God. In fact – Colin just has a heart for people!

Colin is the author of several books, including *Strong Church Foundations*, *Jesus or the Couch*, *The Church and Israel*, Demons, Ghost and Angels, Please Do Not Plant Any More Churches and Building Church with Evangelism.

Sierd de Jong

Sierd was brought up in a Christian home and at the age of 12 chose to dedicate his life to God. He already had the desire to work for God. In his home church he served as a cell group leader, youth leader and later became one of the elders. In May 1996, Sierd and his wife, Mirjam, were sent out to start a church and pastor in a village called Zevenhuizen (The Netherlands).

Sierd and Mirjam have three daughters and are part of the MFG leadership team. Sierd has a heart to see strong local churches being built so they can be a strong testimony for the Lord Jesus Christ and produce lasting fruit.

Dick Iverson

Dick Iverson is the Founder of Ministers Fellowship International, and spiritual father to many pastors around the world. He is the founding pastor of Bible Temple (now City Bible Church) in Portland, Oregon, where he pastored for over forty years.

Pastor Iverson's main function is that of apostolic ministry to pastors and church leaders. He has authored eight books and co-authored a ninth.

Chip Kawalsingh

Chip is the senior pastor of Harvest City Church in Leicester, England and is a regular speaker at churches and conferences worldwide. He and his wife Sarah have three children, Brandon, Dylan and Trinity.

Chip is the author of several books, including *An Extra Shot, God, a Mocha & Me*, *Formation Leadership* and *Partnership Guide*.

Memos Sakellariou

Memos has been pastoring since 1979 and has been the senior pastor of a thriving, growing church in Athens, Greece since 1988.

He and his wife Efi were married in 1977 and have one son, two daughters and three grandchildren so far.

Memos has a heart to reach out to other local Greek pastors.

Gordon Tose

Gordon joined Huddersfield Christian Fellowship and its pastor, Colin Cooper, in 1988, three years after becoming a Christian.

He came onto the church staff in 1991, became an elder in 1993 and since then has developed a real understanding of how the local church functions. His particular areas of interest are church government, support leadership and relationships generally, and he has taught extensively on these subjects both in the UK and abroad.

Gordon is married to Marjorie and has two married sons, both of whom are part of the Fellowship. They have three grandchildren so far.

Gordon is the author of several books, including *Support Ministry, Covenant Relationships, Godly Authority and Going The Distance.*

Anthony Tselentakis

Anthony and his wife Linda pastor a church in Thessaloniki, Greece, that was birthed ten years ago from a small home group. Anthony is a dynamic preacher, a man of faith and is passionate for the Word of God and the church of Jesus Christ.

Anthony works especially with the younger generation and his aim is to reach, train and disciple young people.

Anthony and Linda have been blessed with two sons who are fully involved with them in the church.

About Ministers Fellowship Global

Ministers Fellowship Global (MFG) is an organisation which supports pastors and elders and is based on relationships.

MFG exists to facilitate and nurture meaningful relationships amongst members, equipping and enabling them to be more effective in their calling, for the purpose of building and multiplying strong local churches around the world.

MFG aims to support church leaders by helping them to establish meaningful covenant relationships with like-minded leaders, by providing resources to the ministers to enhance their personal life and ministry, by providing a sense of covering and accountability, by providing for the rejuvenation and refreshing of battle-weary leaders and by giving each member a sense of connection to a larger family network and a worldwide vision.

MFG benefits congregations by assisting their pastors and leaders, giving congregations a sense of national and international identity, providing a sense of security and a place to turn in times of difficulty, and by exposing local congregations to ministries that will help them build.

If you would like to learn more about MFG, please contact us:

Ministers Fellowship Global
Cathedral House
Huddersfield
HD1 3LG
United Kingdom

T: +44 (0)1484 467324

info@ministersfellowshipglobal.com
www.ministersfellowshipglobal.com

Building Churches with APOSTLES and PROPHETS

Ministers Fellowship GLOBAL

Colin Cooper | Sierd de Jong | Dick Iverson | Chip Kawalsingh
Memos Sakellariou | Gordon Tose | Anthony Tselentakis

ISBN 978-0-9561415-5-2
A catalogue record for this book is available from the British Library

First published in the UK in 2012 by Harvest City Publishing

Reprinted 2016 by Cathedral House Media

Design and Layout: Darrell Woods
Cover Design: Marcus Woolcock

Emphasis has been added to some scriptures by the authors. Comments on scripture are clearly indicated as such in the text.

Table of Contents

Chapter 1

What is an Apostle?

Colin Cooper

Over the years, I have heard men refer to themselves as apostles and I have also heard others refer to men as apostles. There has been much discussion about apostles in the Christian world, but I did look up the word 'apostle' in the Concise Oxford Dictionary and to my surprise I could not find it. So the word apostle is little known in today's secular world. So I returned to my personal studies on apostles which I did over 30 years ago.

When John the Baptist died, it was the completion of the Old Testament canon of scripture and the beginning of the New.

There is a school of thought that the 'Apostolic Ministry' died out when the last of the Apostles of the Lamb died. Often the gifts of the Spirit are confused with apostolic function. The scripture that would be given by those who see gifts as having died with the Apostles is 1 Corinthians 13:8. This would be bad hermeneutics because it is dangerous to build a doctrine around one verse of scripture. We should use the whole of the Bible to balance out the whole of the Bible. If this scripture was meant to say that apostles were no longer in existence, then God would be contradicting himself in Ephesians 4:7-13:

> *'Jesus gave apostles, prophets, evangelists, pastors and teachers to prepare God's people for works of service, so that the body of Christ may be built up.'*

Nowhere in the Bible does it say that He took back these gifts!

The 'five-fold ministry' which these gifts are called are not gifts of the Holy Spirit, but gifts from Christ to build His Church. After the ascension of Christ Jesus, He gave the gifts to men. *An apostle is an ascension gift ministry to the Church.*

Now let's look at the word 'apostle' which comes from the Greek 'ἀππόστολος' (*'Apostolos'*). Rome would send ships to establish a colony. They would be called apostles because they were sent.

In English, apostle means 'an emissary'. From the Latin *'mitto'* (send). *An apostle has been sent* – in the Hebrew the word is 'Shalach', meaning 'commissioned by God' and 'given authority by God'.

In Isaiah 6:8, Isaiah heard the voice of the Lord saying, '*Whom shall I send?*' Isaiah responded by saying, '*Send me*'.

In the Septuagint, the word *'apostello'* or *'exapostello'* is used 700 times.

An apostle is clearly a sent one

Are all apostles the same? The answer is *no*, because there are different levels of the apostolic order.

- Hebrews 3:1 talks about Jesus the Apostle and High Priest, so an apostle also applies to the priesthood. Moses, Elijah, Elisha and Ezekiel were all priesthood apostles, but Jesus the Christ was unique because He was also the head of the Church (Colossians 1:18-19).
- The maximum number was Twelve Apostles of the Lamb (Revelation 21:14; Acts 1:13). Luke 6:13 tells us that He called them to Him or He chose them and designated them apostles. Who were they? Simon named Peter was first, then Andrew, James, John, Philip, Bartholomew, Matthew, Thomas, James son of Alphaeus, Simon the Zealot, Judas son of James and divinely placed last was Judas Iscariot who became a traitor. Even with a title like 'Apostle of the Lamb', it did not make men infallible.

- Paul talked about some super apostles in 2 Corinthians 11:5 (NIV). In the Authorised Version they are called chief apostles, to which Paul said, *'I am not inferior to these'*.

Acts 1:25 tells us that after Judas, another apostle was needed to take over from him. In Acts 1:26 Matthias was chosen and added to the eleven.

Why did the Apostles choose another?

Why did the Apostles choose another instead of leaving it at eleven apostles? Numbers always have a significant meaning in the Bible. For example, the number six we know as the anti-Christ and the number of man; number seven is perfection; number eight is Jesus and number twelve is the number of government.

Revelation 21 describes the fantastic New Jerusalem, the City of the Living God. In verse 12 it talks about twelve gates, twelve angels and twelve tribes of Israel.

The number twelve is the number of government

- Genesis 48-49 talks about Jacob's twelve sons, who were the foundation for Israel.
- Exodus 15:27 talks about the twelve wells of water, which were symbolic of apostles.
- Leviticus 24:5 talks about the twelve loaves of shew bread.
- 1 Kings 10:20 talks about the twelve lions of Solomon's throne.
- Exodus 24:4 talks about the twelve pillars of stone on Mount Sinai, symbolic of twelve apostles.
- Exodus 28:21 talks about the twelve stones representing the twelve tribal names of Israel.
- 1 Kings 7, verses 25 and 44 talk about the twelve bulls which held up the sea over them.
- 1 Chronicles 26:13-19 talks about the twelve portals at Jerusalem's gate.
- Numbers 7 talks about the twelve leaders who brought offerings at the temple's dedication.

Twelve is the number throughout the Bible that speaks of government.

Paul the Apostle was different or unique because he was not mentioned as one of the Twelve. Paul writes about the Twelve in 1 Corinthians 15:5, and verses 8-10 says, '*last of all he appeared to me also as to one abnormally born. For I am the least of the apostles and do not even deserve to be called an apostle*'. Peter was called to be an apostle to the Jews and Paul was called to be an apostle to the Gentiles. In 2 Peter 3:15-16, Peter describes Paul and his sayings as hard to understand, but he accepted them as he believed they were inspired by God.

In 1 Corinthians 11:23, Paul said, '*For I received from the Lord what I also passed on to you*'. Notice he did not say 'what I received from other apostles'. He did not get revelation from them.

Paul was unique and different from the other apostles. He was the first post-ascension apostle chosen by Christ from Heaven under the new dispensation of the Spirit.

Paul's post-ascension apostleship was validated like no other apostle because all the others were lesser apostles.

Apart from the original Twelve Apostles, another sixteen were added: Matthias (Acts 1:26), James, the brother of Jesus (Galatians 1:19), Barnabas and Paul (Acts 14:14), Apollos (1 Corinthians 4:6-9), Andronicus and Junias (Romans 16:7), Epaphroditus (Philippians 2:25), Titus, plus two unnamed apostles (2 Corinthians 8:23), Timothy and Erastus (Acts 19:22), Judas and Silas (Acts 15:22) and Tychicus (2 Timothy 4:12).

And *in* the Church, God has appointed first of all apostles. In 1 Corinthians 12:28, *Jesus* (not the Holy Spirit) gave apostles to the Church. In the New Testament, twenty-eight apostles were mentioned in total.

No apostle compared with Paul in his revelation, signs, wonders and miracles. All other apostles were lesser apostles.

What are the qualifications of an apostle?

1. Humbleness

Paul never used the word apostle as a title. Paul understood the words of Jesus in Matthew 23:6-10: '*do not be called Rabbi* (an ecclesiastical title) *or Master*'. This would translate today as 'don't be called Apostle Smith or Dr. Jones or Evangelist Brown'.

Titles come from the Babylonian church:

Holy Father – Your Excellency – Your Holiness

Deborah was called a mother in Israel not Mother Superior (Judges 5:7). Reverend is a title much used today, but scripture says to revere His name, not ours.

The Salvation Army Captain: The Bible says there is only one captain and He is the Captain of the Lord of Hosts.

'Apostle' and 'bishop' were never intended to be titles, only a description of the function.

Paul, who was an apostle or Bill, who happens to be a pastor.

John 5:44 and 12:43 warn us about taking praise from men more than from God.

Apostles worked with other men

In the New Testament Church, an apostle was not a loner or independent of other ministries. I have often asked men with the title of apostle, 'Where are you accountable?' or 'Who are you accountable to?' The answer has often been a church or a place, but on further inspection it is only a name. They are often not planted in, or a member of, that church. Paul the Apostle was *under authority.* In Acts 13:3, he had hands laid on him by the leaders of the church in Antioch; they sent him out.

In Acts 8, Peter and John were sent to Samaria to help Philip the Evangelist. Paul and Silas worked together, Barnabas and Saul, Judas and Silas.

Apostles are not the most important team players

In this modern age we have seen the men called apostles in the top position in leadership, and the reason for this comes from 1 Corinthians 12:28: '*And in the church God has appointed first of all apostles, second prophets, third teachers, then workers of miracles*'. From this we have placed the apostle on a throne, but hermeneutically this is not what the text is saying.

If I were to go to the local DIY store to buy tools to fix my garden shed and I thought, 'What do I need? First of all nails, then some glue and a hammer and finally wood', that does not make the nails the most important item in the store. They are just a part of the whole. Apostles are a part of the whole but are not meant to be the *lord of all.* They are part of a team and the team is better off with an apostle's gifting functioning in it.

2. A character qualification of an elder

Peter said he was a fellow elder among you (1 Peter 5:1), so Peter was an elder among elders. Paul gave the character qualification of an elder in 1 Timothy 3:1-7. This list of qualifications would disqualify most modern apostles.

Paul again laid out the qualifications of an elder in Titus 1:5-9. So these scriptures are a firm measuring rod to discern who is an apostle and who has only the title of an apostle.

3. Patience

Ouch, has that just disqualified you? 2 Corinthians 12:12 lists the things that mark an apostle, but we tend to notice the miracle part only, rather than '*These were done among you with great perseverance*'. This is a missing attribute in many gift men today.

4. A servant spirit

How does a man or woman become great? Mark 10:43-45 tells us that it's by becoming a servant and being a slave of all, '*For even the Son of Man did not come to be served but to serve*'. Many modern day apostles have people pandering to their needs and the saints become their servants. Now I am not saying that we do not honour those over us because when we honour our leaders we get blessed by doing so, but having saints run after us is not the Bible view of an apostle.

5. A father in the Lord

1 Corinthians 4:15 states that there are not many fathers but many gift men. Paul referred to himself as a father (Philippians 2:22). In 1 Thessalonians 2:6-8, Paul talked about his love for the flock, and in verse 11 he explains how he dealt with people as a father with his children.

6. An excellent example

Paul was confident that he had been the best example of Christ-likeness in 1 Corinthians 11:1. He said, '*Follow my example as I follow the example of Christ*'. I have seen young men follow the example of modern apostles and it has caused pain because the named apostle was not a good example to follow.

7. Government and authority

Many modern apostles have ruled very harshly over churches and leaders and have caused pain and damage. Paul had a clear understanding as to how authority should be exercised. In 2 Corinthians 1:24, Paul said, '*Not that we Lord it over your faith, but we work with you for your joy*'. An apostle works for edification and not destruction.

Paul was firm about sin. In 2 Corinthians 13:2, he said, '*I already gave you a warning when I was with you the second time. I now repeat it while absent: on my return I will not spare those who sinned earlier or any of the others*'. Paul was not in the camp of modern day apostles with an imbalanced view of grace.

8. Firm doctrinal beliefs

Titus 1:9 says, '*encourage others by sound doctrine and refute those who oppose it*'. This is a mark of a true apostle. He is not blown around by the latest trends to hit the churches (Ephesians 4:14). In fact, Acts 2:42 says that the saints were devoted to the Apostles' teaching. So a true apostle does not bend with the fads.

9. Unconditional love

So many of today's apostles are men who will cut you off or disown you if you make a mistake. How did Paul view his relationship with others? 2 Corinthians 12:15 expresses some of his heart on love, and listen to what he says in 1 Corinthians 13:4-8: '*Love is patient, love is kind. It does not envy, it does not boast, it is not proud*'. He then gives an understanding to us as to how love functions. May the Lord raise up many more genuine apostles.

How does an apostle function?

An apostle will function in the grace given to him, so his function is in various degrees. Ephesians 4:11 gives us a glimpse of this function:

- To mature the saints.
- To release people into their gifting.
- To build up the Church body.
- To make the saints more like Christ.
- To bring the saints to the unity of faith.
- An apostle will help establish the local church (all who do this are not necessarily apostles). An apostle will give the local church a good foundation.
- An apostle has a revelation of scripture and teaches it (1 Timothy 2:7). In 2 Timothy 1:11, Paul was appointed to be a herald and teacher.
- Signs and wonders will accompany a true apostle (Acts 5:12).
- Apostles will set in ministries (Acts 6:1-6; Acts 14:23).
- Church judgement, along with discipline, will be an apostle's function and he will also settle disputes. Examples are found in Acts 5:1-11 (Ananias and Sapphira), Acts 13:8-11 (Elymas the sorcerer) and 1 Timothy 1:20 (Hymenaeus and Alexander, false doctrine).
- Apostles had great vision for the Church (Ephesians 3:1-9; Ephesians 4:1-16).
- Unlike modern day ministries, New Testament apostles were willing to suffer for the Church (Acts 5:18-40). Also, in Colossians Paul talks about the pressure while continuing in the faith (Colossians 1:23-29).
- Apostles have been tested and proven to be true (Acts 17:10-12; Revelation 2:2).

Apostles have a unique ability. They are also gifted with the whole of the five-fold ministry as listed in Ephesians 4:11. They prophesy, teach, evangelise and pastor. This builds the House of the Lord and gives it an excellent foundation.

True apostles will be found in a local church. In fact, an apostle must be in a local church.

An apostle makes the House of the Lord safe, secure and fun.

Chapter 2

False Apostles and Ministries

Colin Cooper

I have seen many men in my time serving the Church and they have come with many titles. One of these titles has been frequently used, it is the title 'Apostle'.

There are many books describing what an apostle is, but we struggle to find a book which describes what a false apostle is, and there are many.

I once worked with a man who claimed to be an apostle, when I was very young and naïve. This apostle was an amazing preacher who captivated his listeners, he ruled over a large church, and a moderate-sized movement and once a year had a huge gathering of churches and leaders.

Year by year, this movement grew and drew many in from the denominations who were looking for something more like the Kingdom the Bible spoke about, and this apostle seemed to be God's man with the answer.

Slowly, people began to disappear from the organisation. They were later traced and found not to be going to church because of harsh treatment by the apostle. Then from a trickle of people leaving, it became many. Not only individuals, but whole churches were damaged, split and hurt.

Now, was this the work of an apostle? Let's remind ourselves about the qualifications of an apostle: humility, good character, patience, a servant, a father, an example and unconditional love. None of these were exhibited by this particular apostle.

The two ingredients exhibited on this occasion were a firm doctrinal belief and authority. So without the other qualifications, authority and doctrine can be destructive.

Does the Bible say anything about false apostles?

In 2 Corinthians 11:12-13, Paul talks about men who seek to be equal with the Apostles and boast about what they do. *They are false apostles.*

Revelation 2:2 talks about having tested those who *claim to be* apostles but are not, and have *found them false.*

This is not talking about their gift, as they would certainly function in their gifting, but this is talking about *self-appointed* apostles.

Self-appointed

In Numbers 16 and 17, we have two examples of self-appointment. The first example is Korah. Let's look at the steps to self-appointment.

In Numbers 16:2, they were community leaders, they had been given responsibility. In Numbers 16:3, they came as a group to oppose the leader, Moses. They were self-appointed God's policemen, and said to Moses, '*The whole community is holy, everyone of them*' – in other words, 'we know as much as you'.

Perhaps they were as holy as Moses, they may have known as much as Moses; they had been appointed as leaders and were well known.

What did God think about all this? Numbers 16:31-33 tell us that the ground opened up and swallowed them. Why? The ground swallowed them because they had appointed themselves to confront God's man, or the main leader.

Not satisfied with the position they had been given, they continually wanted more authority. This, of course, was the same problem Paul faced in 2 Corinthians 11:12-13. Men wanting equality will put titles on themselves and lay hands on themselves.

In Numbers 17, men grumbled against the leadership, but the Lord said in verse 10 'they grumble against *me*'. In Jude verse 11, the Lord called Cain, Balaam, and Korah rebellious. Self-appointed ministries may be gifted but that does not qualify them to do the job they want to be recognised for.

When I was 17, I wanted my friends to go to a discotheque (as they called them in the '60s). The disco was in the next town. My friends wanted to go to a local disco but I persuaded them to go to the next town so we all went. Why did they change their minds? Because I had leadership qualities. I was not a Christian but I had a gift. Many self-appointed apostles have gifting, but it is human ability rather than God inspired activity.

Never follow a man because he is gifted

Matthew 7:22 says, '*did we not prophesy in your name, and in your name drive out demons and perform many miracles?*' This sounds like Holy Ghost ministry, but in verse 23 the Lord calls them '*evildoers*', and says, '*I never knew you*'. The Lord never contradicted them, He was saying 'I don't have any intimacy with you'. This was an example of false ministry.

True and false ministry

True	False
Loves the Church	Hurts the Church and can cause a split which he will say was divinely inspired
Patience with people	Gets irritated when people question him
A good character	Continually hear bad reports about him
A fathering heart	Gives rules to live by

cont.

True	**False**
Gentle in authority	Gives hard judgments
A firm doctrine	Changes views continually with new doctrines or fads
Loves unconditionally	He is pragmatic and drops people if he thinks they are no longer useful
Humble in spirit	Boasts about his achievements
Approachable	Hard to connect with or reach
Fully part of the Church	He is aloof
Gives advice and direction	Controls situations
A team player	Has a subservient committee
Works through staff difficulties	Fires staff if they cause difficulties
Releases people into ministry	Uses people to make him look good
Sacrifices financially	Believes large cars, houses and having money is a sign of God's blessing
Builds relationships	An opportunist
Balanced ministry	Seeks phenomena

An apostle of the Lord builds with an Isaac spirit. A false apostle will have an Ishmael spirit. One builds with the Spirit of the Lord and the other with a carnal, human spirit. Both get results.

I have travelled to many countries and continents and observed the real and the false in many things, including those who would name the name of Christ.

In the wonderful country of India you see many amazing things. Sri-Sathya Sai Baba was a famous Indian spiritual leader who died recently. He built hospitals, schools, health centres and he cared for people. At the age of 14 he declared to his parents that he had come to the world to establish righteousness and to bring love to mankind. Sri-Sathya Sai Baba declared 'there is only one God'. Sounds good!

Prime ministers, presidents, movie stars and professional men and women sought him out. They came from all over the world to be motivated for God and fellow man. He offered an ocean of knowledge and spiritual guidance and he quoted that it is not necessary to read all scripture, only to put into practice his spiritual teaching.

He could make money appear from the air, he could make jewellery form in front of him, he could touch people who had serious illnesses and they would be healed in front of peoples' eyes, but he did not believe in salvation through Christ. His teaching was not remotely based on the Bible, but he was an Indian mystic with real supernatural powers. This is the same source that some who call themselves apostles use today in the western world.

Sometimes the big names we love to hear preaching are found to be living in immorality. Many Christians then become disillusioned because they believed in them. Men can preach excellently, perform miracles and have great personalities, but they have simply moved in the flesh which produces something looking like the Spirit of God but it is not. Galatians 5:24-25 tells us that those who belong to Christ have crucified the sinful nature and keep in step with the Spirit.

Soul or Spirit?

'*The first man Adam became a living being*' (1 Corinthians 15:45), the last Adam, a life-giving Spirit. In other words, Adam became a living soul. In the Hebrew it says Adam became '*nephesh*'. But the last Adam, which is Jesus, was a life giving spirit, or '*ruach*' in the Greek.

So it is possible for an apostle to move in the *nephesh* (soul) but unless he moves in the *ruach* (spirit or wind) then ultimately it produces chaos and spiritual death.

If you see signs and wonders from anyone, especially those who claim to be apostles (2 Corinthians 11:13; Revelation 2:2), ask is it *ruach* or *nephesh* signs, wonders and miracles?

John 12:24-25 tells us that a seed buried in the ground will die, but then it produces many more seeds. Then in verse 25 it compares this to a man. If that man loses his life, he will keep it for all eternity. A man, like the seed, has to die to his ambitions, and if he dies he will keep his life in the next world.

Unless apostolic gifts, or any other gift men, die to the *nephesh* and allow the *ruach* to live, then he falls into the same category as Matthew 7:23: '*I never knew you. Away from me, you evildoers!*'

Let the soulish man in us die. When we die to ourselves then we produce much more fruit.

Nephesh or *ruach*? Practical observations of a false apostle

1. *A false apostle does build*, but he does not have a building permit from God.

   Genesis 11:1-8 speaks about false building. In verse 3, they used brick instead of stone and bitumen for mortar. The building looked good but wasn't built according to God's plan. This is a shadow of a false apostle.

   In verse 4, they built for themselves, not for others. Like a false apostle, it was for their own benefit.

   In 1 Corinthians 3:10, Paul the Apostle said, '*each one should be careful how he builds*'.
2. *A false apostle will speak of unity.* In Genesis 11:6 the Lord said, '*If as one people speaking the same language they have begun to do this, then nothing they plan to do will be impossible for them*'.

   When God is not in something, a false apostle can build with a false unity but ultimately people get scattered because the shepherd was not genuine.
3. A false apostle will try and gather as many people as possible, no matter what the quality is like. The more people, the more successful he looks. He will tell others to leave the group they are in and join him.

   In John 6:37, Jesus said, '*All that the Father gives me will come to me*'. A true apostle would never grab people or persuade them to join him but would only have what the Father gives.
4. A false apostle will have a history of broken relationships. In his secular employment he will more than likely have left many jobs with disagreement. As he was in the secular, so will he be in the spiritual.
5. A false apostle will have many people link with him because of his gifting and personality, but many leave him and his organisation broken, disappointed and damaged.
6. A false apostle is not accountable to anyone for his actions. Although he may claim to be accountable, no one dare speak into his life or address his destructive actions.

7. A false apostle will claim to have relationships but they are mainly on a business level. He generally never has a good laugh with friends, watches a movie, chills or does normal fun things that might make him vulnerable.
8. A false apostle likes to give the impression that he is a superstar. He does not want anyone to see that he has weaknesses, can make mistakes, or has need of others. But he is pretentious, just like the ministries described in Mark 12:38-40.
9. A false apostle will keep people dependant on him rather than making them totally dependent on Jesus.

The Bible warns us about false ministries

Mark 13:22 says, '*For false Christs and false prophets will appear*'.

So why do Christians follow false apostles?

The Bible refers to believers as sheep. Some talk about believers as *Ekklesia*, 'the called out ones.' That is great teaching but hard to understand, but when believers are called sheep I understand that. 'Sheep' is mentioned 500 times in the Bible.

1. Sheep really are dumb, not bright animals at all.
2. They are weak creatures with no weapons like teeth or claws.
3. They often get lost and get into bad situations.
4. They need a shepherd who can lovingly guide them.

This description of Christians tells us why they can be so easily deceived and follow someone they think they can trust.

If a person is desperately sick and someone promises healing, they will follow, especially if a person has a title like 'Apostle' and tells them that they can have their life improved.

If prophecies are given and we like the prophecy, the average Christian will follow it. But when it is false, we can be easily deceived, and ultimately Christians under false ministries can be disillusioned and often stop going to church altogether. They really are like lost sheep.

But they perform miracles!

One thing I said earlier is never follow a man because of his gift, and again I remind you of Matthew 7:21-23. When amazing Ephesians 4 type ministries were in action but the Lord rejected them because they had no intimate relationship with Him, the supernatural acts were real, but the individuals were false.

I will try to give a panoramic glimpse across the centuries of the Bible as to how we see real miracles performed by men, but God is not in them.

1 Thessalonians 5:23 talks about the spirit, soul and body. The body we understand, the spirit is often written about, preached about and talked about, but when it comes to the soul, little is taught, spoken or written. So let's have a glimpse over the centuries about men's concepts of the soul.

- Platonism: In 429-347 BC, mankind believed in a pre-existent life, this was called Platonism. The belief was that souls enjoyed a higher existence prior to the human body. In a pre-cosmic fall, souls transmigrated to human bodies which is called 'metempsychosis'. Now soul and body co-existed.

  Human and animal souls passed through more than one body in a progressive purification. The early Church discussed metempsychosis and fought each other over the belief. There was a similarity to the Christian belief on the resurrection of the body.
- Neoplatonism: Centuries later, a group called Neoplatonists (from Plato) of the Italian Renaissance came from a place called Lassing. They had a group emerge from them who were spiritists and theosophists who believed in the soul's supremacy. Out of this came the cult of Swedenborganism, headed by Emanuel Swedenborg (1688-1772).
- Traducianism: Traducianism (or generationism) believed that the body and soul came from our parents by the process of procreation.

  Traducianism became the doctrine of the Lutherans as God moved to bring the Church back to its original plan.

- Creationism: Creationism is a doctrine that believes God created man as body, soul and spirit. As Ephesians 4:24 and Colossians 3:10 suggest, we are created to be like God in the image of the Creator. But when Adam sinned the fall came, and in Genesis 46:27 it talks about Jacob and souls that came out of his loins (Septuagint).

  In Acts 2:4, those that received word of Him were baptised, about 3000 souls (interlinear). This doctrine is more acceptable to Christians. Genesis 6:3 says that after the fall, man became mortal or a living soul.

Groups with supernatural acts:

- Buddhism: Gautama Siddharta (who was an atheist) believed in the soul and that it would transmigrate to Nirvana, which is a state of blessedness. He predicted the future and performed magic. He broke physical boundaries to release the soul. Today, many famous people are Buddhist-believing, because of supernatural acts.
- Psychometry: Allows the mind to be free from the body.
- Pathetism: Gets the mind to withdraw from consciousness of pain.
- Telepathy: When a man can use psychic force to know another's mind.
- Spiritism: People with hunchbacks and other illnesses have genuinely been healed.
- Clairvoyance: Where individuals see, hear and smell things thousands of miles away.
- Taoism: Abstract meditation where the soul rules the body.
- Unity Club: Have abstract meditation and each degree entered has its own light with new truth.
- Christian Science (which is not Christian): Invented by Mary Baker Eddy, it trains the mind and will to be free from sickness with confirmed medical healings.
- Christian sects and cults have seen much in the way of miracles and healings.

How do we see miracles without God?

Satan can appear to cause pain and misery in Africa, Europe, the USA, Asia and to individuals all over the world at exactly the same time. How can this be?

Satan is simply a fallen angel and can only be in one place at a time but appears to be in many places at the same time. True, he has other fallen angels with him, but only one third. Not enough to cause trouble to every individual on the earth.

Revelation 18:11-14 gives us some of the answers. This is a chapter about the spirit of Babylon which we will see in the last days. It is a time of economic co-operation in the world, a real global village. But note verse 13; not only is there great commerce but there is trade in the *souls of men*. So in the last days, although Satan is not omnipresent like God, he uses men's souls to work his evil. This gives the appearance that Satan is in many places at the same time.

All of those listed as real supernatural acts are simply Satan using the soul of man.

Matthew 24:24-25 talks about false Christs or false anointing, warning us before they appear so we are not deceived. 2 Thessalonians 2:8-11 warns of counterfeit signs, wonders and miracles; many will be and are deceived by supernatural acts in this generation of ours.

- Never follow a man because of good preaching.
- Never follow a man because of gifting.
- Never follow a man because of a nice personality.
- Never follow a man because of signs and wonders.
- Never follow a man because he has the title of an apostle.

How then do we decide who is a genuine apostle?

Many apostles simply have the title because they have appointed themselves and laid hands on themselves.
Far better that somebody else tells you what you are rather than you claim to be something.

Philippians 2:19-24 talks about the relationship between Timothy and the Apostle Paul. It was an intimate relationship. Timothy knew the lifestyle of Paul.

In 2 Timothy 1:2, Paul the Apostle called Timothy '*my dear son*', even though Timothy was by now in his 40s. It was a transparent, deep relationship. '*My dear son*' was more than a working relationship.

In 2 Timothy 3:10, Paul said to Timothy, '*You, however, know all about my teaching, my way of life*'. The word 'know' is the same as the Lord used in Matthew 7:23 when He said, '*I never knew you*' or 'I had no intimacy with you'. So Paul and Timothy had a deep, intimate relationship.

- An apostle will be approachable and have close friends.
- You must get to know and build a relationship with any apostle before you sacrifice your life to him.
- You must know that his teaching is not rhetoric but a lifestyle that he lives.
- It involves accountability. In 2 Timothy 3:10, Paul said '*You, however, know all about my teaching, my way of life*'. Paul was an open-spirited man.
- In 2 Timothy 2:2, Paul put into Timothy that he should only trust people who were faithful. Faithfulness comes out of long-term relationships.

You recognise a true apostle because he is a father, like Paul was to Timothy. An apostle has a fathering mentality.

Remember, the soul can reproduce something that looks like the Spirit of the Lord, and many apostles reproduce miracles that come from the soul, and they deceive people.

In John 3:6, Jesus said, '*Flesh* (soul) *gives birth to flesh, but the Spirit gives birth to the spirit*'. Only the things birthed in the Holy Spirit will last. In fact, many titled 'Apostle' move in the flesh, but it is very attractive and many are open to deception.

Recognising an apostle

An apostle sent by the Lord is vital to help build the Church of Jesus Christ. God is intimately involved with His apostles. The Lord will determine how long an apostle will function and how much influence he has. Paul was recognised as an apostle in Antioch but not in Jerusalem. In 1 Corinthians 9:2, '*Even though I may not be an apostle to others, surely I am to you! For you are the seal of my apostleship in the Lord*', said Paul.

- Some apostles are local.
- Some apostles are national.
- Some apostles are international.
- Some groups may receive an apostle when others would not.
- An apostle must know that he is called by God and to whom he is called.
- His own leaders must recognise him as an apostle rather than be self-appointed.
- His own base church should recognise him as an apostle.
- An apostle will never impose his rule on any person, church or organisation. He is not a dictator (1 Corinthians 16:12; 1 Peter 5:2).
- Other apostles of proven credibility will also recognise him.
- An apostle must be based and be accountable in a local church.
- He must be a proven church builder.
- An apostle will have sons in the Lord.

Jesus was the Chief Apostle

Jesus was sent by His Father to accomplish an eternal plan (Hebrews 3:1; John 3:16; 20:21).

Levels of the apostles

The Twelve Apostles of the Lamb

The Twelve Apostles were unique, chosen by Jesus (Luke 6:12-16). They are mentioned in Revelation 21:14: '*The wall of the city had twelve foundations, and on them were the names of the twelve apostles of the Lamb*'. The Apostles of the Lamb will never happen again. They were a bridge from the old-time prophets to the Church of Jesus.

The post-ascension apostles

The post-ascension apostles are another level of apostle. Ephesians 4 tells us that this level of apostles came after Jesus ascended and this group was to bring the saints to a level of unity and to the stature and fullness of Jesus (Ephesians 4:13).

1 Corinthians 12:28 tells us that without apostles the Church would not have all the ingredients to function correctly. Here is a list of this level of apostles as described in the Bible:

- Apollos (1 Corinthians 4:6, 9).
- Titus (2 Corinthians 8:23).
- Epaphroditus (Philippians 2:25).
- Silas (1 Thessalonians 1:1; 2:7).
- Timothy (1 Thessalonians 1:1; 2:7).
- Junias (Romans 16:7).
- Andronicus (Romans 16:7).
- Barnabas (Acts 4:36; 13:2; 14:14).
- James, who was the brother of Jesus (Galatians 1:19).

Apostolic ministry

Some who did an apostolic work were not given the title of apostle. For example, Jesus sent out the 70 who did the same kind of work as the Twelve Apostles of the Lamb. Many church planters today in the twenty first century are doing an apostolic work but *they are not apostles*, however they would be part of the Ephesians 4 ministries.

All apostles have gone through the fires of testing.

Here is a rough diagram as to how the apostle is shaped:

Saved Changed	Called A seed	Testings Perseverance	Beginnings Functioning	Released Fruitfulness

The man who has been called needs to be like clay in the potter's hand:

- The clay is rescued from the ground.
- The clay is pummelled to get all the flaws out that would mar the future vessel.
- The clay is then shaped after going through a process.
- The untried vessel is then placed in the kiln (in the fires).
- The result is a useful, well shaped, rounded vessel.
- Isaiah 64:8 tells us that the Father is the potter and we are the work of His hands.

An apostle will have gone through a tough process to mould him into the father that he is today. Many men today have megachurches, but they themselves are not apostles as they have not gone through the refining fires and often the church has been handed down to them and they have proved to be good managers and orators.

In conclusion, following a man because of gifting or miracles or some new trend is not advisable.

Acts 17:21 talks about the Athenians, who spent their time talking about and listening to the latest ideas.

In Acts 17:11, Paul and Silas were sent by the brothers to Berea. What they found was a group of noblemen. Why were they noble? Because they received the message that was brought to them with great eagerness, but not blindly accepting what was said. They examined the scriptures daily *to see if what the Apostle Paul said was true.* That is a noble group of men.

So we can be like the Athenians and believe what self-appointed men say, or we can be like the Bereans and measure everything by the Word.

Be a Word based people. Any ministry or supernatural act is simply to point men and women to Jesus.

Chapter 3
New Testament Prophets
Sierd de Jong

> *'Now there were these prophets and teachers in the church at Antioch...'* (Acts 13:1, NET)

There is an old Dutch saying: 'What a farmer doesn't know (or what he has not grown or raised himself), he doesn't eat'. What it means is that people tend to stay away from things they are unfamiliar with.

In the church world today, people are familiar with pastors, evangelists and teachers, but not with apostles and even less so with prophets. The theology of most Christians says that the ministry of the prophet was for Old Testament times only and ceased to operate when New Testament times began. Because of this, prophetic ministries are often not found in local churches and if they are, function in ways which do not necessarily conform to the biblical pattern and lack balance.

This should not, and does not, need to be the case. Prophecy and the ministry of the prophet are too precious and too powerful to neglect or throw away (1 Timothy 1:18). The New Testament clearly shows that prophecy and the ministry of the prophet is still intact today (Acts 13:1; 15:32). The ministry of the New Testament prophet cannot be ignored if the church wants to grow to maturity and to its full stature in Christ Jesus (Ephesians 4:11-16).

In this chapter, we are going to look at the ministry of the prophet in a New Testament setting. We are also going to look at the different levels of prophecy and at the biblical guidelines that should be respected in order for prophecy, and the ministry of the prophet, to edify the church instead of destroying it.

What is prophecy?

Prophecy is speaking the mind of God concerning a person, a church or a situation, pertaining to the present or the future.

When it pertains to the present, the nature of prophecy becomes forth-telling. It speaks the mind of God concerning a present situation or concerning what a person or a church is presently going through. It can give insight into why things are the way they are, and it can give answers as to how to handle things in that particular case.

When it pertains to the future, prophecy becomes fore-telling. It speaks the mind of God concerning the future. It can give insight into what God is about to do in that situation or in a person's life, or in the life of a church. This helps that person or church to expect and believe God for the things that have been spoken, and to learn what to do to achieve those things.

> *'Timothy, my son, the instructions I am giving you are based on what some prophets once said about you. If you follow these instructions, you will fight like a good soldier.'* (1 Timothy 1:18, CEV)

Acknowledging the different levels of prophecy

To clearly understand the ministry of the prophet in a New Testament setting, it is very important that we recognise and acknowledge that in the New Testament there are different levels of prophecy.

The best way to explain it is to compare the levels of prophecy to the roles in a hospital. Everyone who works in a hospital has a different level of responsibility. Each level has its boundaries, which should be respected by the person who is acting at that particular level of responsibility.

Firstly, there are the cleaners who are responsible for cleaning the hospital. Although cleaning the hospital is vital and by no means an inferior responsibility, it doesn't take years of education to become a cleaner. After being instructed on how to go about a certain way of working, someone can begin cleaning the hospital quite quickly.

Next, there are the nurses who are responsible for taking care of the patients. It takes a higher measure of expertise to be a nurse than it takes to be a cleaner. That is why it takes a couple of years of studying to become a nurse, and besides that, it takes practical training in how to handle patients while they are sick or recovering. The training is necessary because of the responsibility that goes with being a nurse. For example, nurses have the responsibility of handing out medication to patients. It would be irresponsible for a hospital to let people who don't have the proper training do this kind of job because the consequences could be far-reaching.

Then there are the surgeons who are responsible for operating on patients. It takes an even greater measure of expertise to be a surgeon than it does to be a nurse or a cleaner. It takes several more years of training to become a surgeon. Again, more, and better, training is required because of the increased responsibility that goes with being a surgeon. Human life is directly at stake here.

Can you imagine a hospital that does not know or respect the different levels of responsibility? Can you imagine a hospital that allows the cleaners to hand out the medicines? And allows the nurses to operate on the patients? Can you imagine the problems that it would create in the lives of so many people? Personally, I would not want to be treated in a hospital that doesn't know or recognise the different levels of responsibility.

This is also true for prophecy. When churches do not recognise and respect the different levels of prophecy and allow anyone to prophesy anything to anybody, then lives will be damaged or even destroyed. Just as I would not feel safe in a hospital that doesn't acknowledge the different levels of responsibility, I would not feel safe in a church that doesn't know and acknowledge the different levels of prophecy.

When the different levels are not respected, prophecy can become destructive. When used correctly, it can be powerful and edifying.

Prophecy is like fire and water in the home. When they're respected and used correctly they are a great blessing; you can drink from the tap and you can cook from the stove. But used incorrectly, those same elements have the power and potential to damage or even destroy the house.

The different levels of prophecy

'All of this makes us even more certain that what the prophets said is true. So you should pay close attention to their message, as you would to a lamp shining in some dark place. You must keep on paying attention until daylight comes and the morning star rises in your hearts. But you need to realize that no one alone can understand any of the prophecies in the Scriptures. The prophets did not think these things up on their own, but they were guided by the Spirit of God.' (2 Peter 1:19-20, CEV)

Before we look at the different levels of prophecy, it is important to note that the Bible is the absolute highest level of prophecy. All prophecy should be tested against the Word of God, because whilst all other prophecy is fallible, the Word of God is infallible.

Next to the Bible, there are three levels from which someone can prophesy: the spirit of prophecy; the gift of prophecy; and the office of a prophet. Each level has biblical guidelines that should be honoured in order for prophecy to edify the Body of Christ instead of breaking it down. Again, it is like in a hospital: Each level of responsibility has boundaries which must be respected in order to help the patient recover and which, if ignored, could cause harm.

The spirit of prophecy

'Then I fell at his feet to worship him. But he said, "Don't do that! I'm a servant just like you and your brothers and sisters who hold firmly to the witness of Jesus. Worship God! The witness of Jesus is the spirit of prophecy!"' (Revelation 19:10, CEB)

All genuine prophecy flows through the Holy Spirit, who is the spirit of prophecy. Prophesying through the spirit of prophecy happens when a person is inspired by the Holy Spirit to say or do something through which the reality of Jesus is manifested.

Every believer is able to prophesy from this level from time to time, especially when the church comes together in Jesus' name. Through the moving of the Holy Spirit, every believer is able to prophesy (1 Corinthians 14:5a, 31a). An example of this type of prophecy is King Saul's experience when he was amongst the prophets. He started to prophesy himself – not because he was a prophet, but because he was touched by the spirit of prophecy (1 Samuel 10:10; 19:20-24). The same was true for the elders of Israel when they were touched by the Spirit which was on Moses, who was a prophet (Numbers 11:24-30).

When someone prophesies through the spirit of prophecy, it doesn't necessarily mean that he or she has the gift of prophecy, or the office of a prophet. They must hold themselves to the biblical guidelines that define this level of prophecy; that is, to edify, to comfort and to encourage (1 Corinthians 14:3).

The gift of prophecy

> *'Performance of miracles to another, prophecy to another, the ability to tell spirits apart to another, different kinds of tongues to another, and the interpretation of the tongues to another.'* (1 Corinthians 12:10, CEB)

When someone who is regularly prophesying through the spirit of prophecy starts to learn what prophecy is and how it functions, and is confirmed by their local church leaders, then the gift of prophecy can develop in that person's life. The gift of prophecy is one of the nine gifts of the Holy Spirit in 1 Corinthians 12. The daughters of Philip had this gift: *'And he had four maiden daughters who had the gift of prophecy'* (Acts 21:9, AMP).

If we want prophecy, whether through the spirit or the gift of prophecy, to be of benefit, then the person who is prophesying must restrain him or herself and conform to the biblical boundaries which are mentioned in 1 Corinthians 14:3: *'Those who prophesy speak to people, building them up, and giving them encouragement and comfort'* (CEB).

Judging prophecy

All prophecy, however it is brought, must be judged because it is fallible (1 Thessalonians 5:19-21). To protect the church from false or strange prophecies, it is wise to judge the prophecy before a person starts to prophesy in the church meeting. This can, for example, be done by only allowing those who have asked permission from the leadership of the local church to prophesy.

Even though someone is prophesying, whether through the spirit of prophecy or through the gift of prophecy, it does not necessarily mean that he or she is a prophet or prophetess.

The office of a prophet

> *'Both Judas and Silas, who were prophets themselves, encouraged and strengthened the brothers with a long speech.'*(Acts 15:32, NET)

When someone is prophesying on a regular basis through the gift of prophecy in a local church setting, within the biblical boundaries of that gift, and is growing in character and leadership gifting, then the office of a prophet can begin to be developed in that person's life – if, that is, the Lord has called that person to be a prophet.

The difference between someone who prophesies through the gift of prophecy and someone who is a prophet is that a prophet can prophesy through the gift that God has given to him, and because of the mantle that is on him. He doesn't have to wait for a special atmosphere in order to prophesy, although such an atmosphere can help him to move in his gift more sharply.

The ministry of a prophet

The ministry of a prophet is part of the five-fold ministry, making it a leadership ministry in the House of God (Ephesians 4:11-12). In other words, prophets are not sitting in the pews. People with the office of a prophet are those who have been through a process of learning and maturing within a local church, and have been recognised and confirmed as prophets by their local leadership and released into leadership roles.

The ministry of a prophet reaches further than the gift of prophecy. It is like a surgeon who is able to go further in his treatment of a patient than a nurse. Biblically speaking, the ministry of the prophet is there to: edify and strengthen the Church (1 Corinthians 14:3; Ephesians 4:11-16; Acts 15:32); comfort (1 Corinthians 14:3); encourage (1 Corinthians 14:3; Ezra 5:1; 6:14); and give direction (Acts 13:1-3).

At this point it is necessary to stress that there is a difference between Old Testament prophets and New Testament prophets. Although the ministry of a prophet in the New Testament is similar in most areas to that of the Old Testament prophets, there is a big difference that changes the dynamics of the ministry of a prophet in the New Testament.

In the Old Testament, the Holy Spirit was not available to every person. He rested only on people whom God had called to a special assignment, like the prophets. It was through the prophets that God spoke to the kings and to the people. If the king or the people wanted to obey God, they did what the prophet said. But in the New Testament it is different. The Holy Spirit has become available to every believer. Every believer can come to God through Jesus Christ and can hear God speak directly to him or herself. This makes the ministry of a New Testament prophet different to the ministry of an Old Testament prophet. What the prophet has said must be judged according to what the Bible says, but also according to what God has revealed to the believer personally (Romans 8:14).

A prophet can speak things to a person which that person doesn't presently understand. This doesn't necessarily mean that what the prophet has said is wrong. It may simply be that that word needs to be put to one side for a period of time until that person is ready and God reveals its meaning. The time will come when the prophecy will make sense and be very valuable to that person.

Another important point that helps to keep the prophetic ministry a blessing is limiting personal prophecy to a local church setting, where the elders of the church are present while the prophecies are being given. Although the believer can judge for him or herself, it is for their own safety that they also have leaders around them who can help to judge, interpret and deal with the prophecy in an objective way.

Sadly, because many people, including those who function in the prophetic ministry, do not discern the concept of the local church, prophecy has often led to more pain than encouragement for individuals and churches. People have been manipulated and become disillusioned by it. Most of this could have been prevented if prophecy had taken place within the biblical boundaries and within a local church setting.

Prophecy is a very valuable tool, and it fulfills a number of other duties: to warn (Acts 21:8-11; 11:27-30); to convict (1 Corinthians 14:3, 24, 25; 1 Samuel 11-12); to bring exhortation and confirmation (Acts 15:22; Ezra 5:1; 6:14); and to bring insight.

A prophet hears God in a special way that can give him insight into God's Word (Ephesians 3:5), but also into people's lives and problems (Acts 21:10-11; 1 Corinthians 14:25). New Testament prophets can also have insight into events that will happen in the future (Acts 11:27-28).

Another role of the prophet is to transfer vision (Proverbs 29:19; Jeremiah 14:14; 23:6). When God wants to do things, then He reveals those things to us. One of the means that God uses to do this is the ministry of the prophet. A prophet can help prepare the way for the Lord (Luke 1:76).

The final responsibility of a prophet is to establish churches and send out ministries (Ephesians 2:20; 3:5). The Apostles worked together with prophets to lay the foundations of the House of God. They also strengthened and edified the churches and were involved in sending out ministries (Acts 13:1-3).

Due to the subjective nature of the ministry of the prophet, prophets don't work on their own but in teams (Acts 11:27-30; 13:1; 1 Corinthians 14:29). This helps to bring the required balance and judgment in this more-or-less subjective ministry.

Warnings concerning the ministry of the prophet

The Lord is specific about what he expects from His prophets. He gives them two clear warnings. Firstly, God warns prophets to exercise self-control (1 Corinthians 14:32). He wants the prophets to use wisdom in communicating what God is showing them, in order for the body of Christ or the individual believer to be edified and strengthened. Secondly, God warns prophets that they must allow their ministry and their prophecies to be judged (1 Corinthians 14:29). Nobody is infallible and the Bible teaches that all prophecy must be judged (1 John 4:1). There are seven questions that should be asked to judge a prophet:

1. Is his ministry in line with the Word of God?
2. Is his ministry done in a good spirit and attitude?
3. Do his prophecies come to pass? (Deuteronomy 18:22)
4. Does he lead a godly life? (Jeremiah 23:15-16)
5. Does the Holy Spirit confirm what is being said? (John 2:20-21)
6. Are his prophecies confirmed by the mouths of two or three witnesses? (2 Corinthians 13:1)
7. Is he based in, and does he work from, a local church? (Acts 13:1-3)

God also warns His people concerning the ministry of the prophet (Matthew 10:41). It is important for the people of God to receive a prophet, otherwise they will block themselves from becoming mature in Christ (Ephesians 4:11-13). The second warning that the Bible gives to the people of God is to be mindful of false prophets.

Both the Old and New Testaments clearly warn us to be on guard for false prophets. Do not judge a ministry only by the presence of signs and wonders. There are false signs and wonders through which the people of God can be mislead (Mark 13:22).

Conclusion

Many people have seen prophecy and the ministry of the prophet functioning in the wrong way, and because of that, they have become disillusioned by prophecy. They tend to stay away from anything that has links to prophecy or prophets, even though those very same gifts are so vital in the Church today. Prophecy and the ministry of the prophet are required in order to take us to a greater level of maturity and to make us as a Church which is fully representative of Jesus Christ.

Jesus was the master prophet, and if we want the Church to be a reflection of Him – not only partially, but totally – then we have to be open to that side of who Jesus is. As the old saying goes: 'Do not throw the baby out with the bathwater'. In other words, we acknowledge that prophecy has been abused and has not functioned as it was intended, but let's not give up on it. Open yourself to the prophetic and the ministry of the prophet, but be careful to ensure that it remains within the biblical boundaries and is only accepted in the safety and security of a local church setting.

Chapter 4

Mentoring and Fathering in the Local Church

Sierd de Jong

'For though you might have ten thousand instructors in Christ, yet you do not have many fathers; for in Christ Jesus I have begotten you through the gospel.' (1 Corinthians 4:14, NKJV)

With the arrival of the Internet, it has become very easy to draw information or instruction from others and yet remain anonymous. You can get all the information you want without having to interact with a single person.

This is not wrong, but when we speak about fathering and mentoring in the local church, we are talking about something more than just being a provider of information or instruction. In this chapter, we will look at what it means to be a father or a mentor in the House of God and to raise up the next generation.

Life, not just information

'The next day, John was there again, and two of his followers were with him. When he saw Jesus walking by, he said, "Here is the

> *Lamb of God!" John's two followers heard him, and they went with Jesus. When Jesus turned and saw them, he asked, "What do you want?" They answered, "Rabbi, where do you live?" The Hebrew word "Rabbi" means "Teacher." Jesus replied, "Come and see!" It was already about four o'clock in the afternoon when they went with Him and saw where He lived. So they stayed on for the rest of the day.'* (John 1:35-39, CEV)

A rabbi taught his followers by letting them move in and live with him in order for them to learn not only from what the rabbi said, but also from how he applied things in his own life. That is why two of John's followers who wanted to follow Jesus asked Him where He lived. They considered Jesus to be a rabbi, and by living with a rabbi, their lives were being transformed.

Unfortunately, in our western society we do not practice this type of education anymore. The Ancient Greek influence on our culture has meant that the manner in which our society educates is primarily concerned with the mind, rather than the heart of the student. The goal of education in our society is often to communicate information which the student must mentally know and understand. It is not geared to reach the heart and bring life – as long as the student knows and understands the information that is taught, he or she is considered to be a good learner.

We use the same approach in our churches. We preach and teach biblical truths to a group of people and we think that this is all they need in order for them to change and become all that God wants them to be.

I do not want to undermine or play down the awesome power of preaching and teaching the Word of God, but simply preaching and teaching will often not get the job of changing a person's heart and attitudes done thoroughly or reliably.

A far greater impact is made on a person when they can build a personal relationship with a mentor and interaction is regular and on-going between student and mentor, who must invest himself in his student. The mentor needs to let the student come close to him in order for the student to see the principles working in his life. Seeing the principles functioning in the life of the mentor will have a great impact on the student's life. The mentor's example helps the student to make the principles that are taught an integral part of his or her own life. This way of learning helps to ensure that the lessons are learnt and enacted to be life-changing and permanent.

The mentor serves as an example or role-model for the student of who he or she wants to become in life. The student watches especially how his or her mentor handles hard times and seemingly impossible situations.

As a role-model, the mentor should be focused, first and foremost, on being a godly person. He doesn't have to be perfect - there are no perfect mentors and no perfect students, just as there are no perfect fathers and no perfect children – but he has to show his student what it means to be a servant of God by being a good personal example of this.

For the student to really enjoy being mentored, and to make the most of his or her relationship with the mentor, he or she needs to be sincere. Sincerity is an important key to becoming what he or she desires to be. The student needs the sincerity and the willingness to change and to put the information he or she receives into practice.

As stated earlier, in our society a person is considered to have learnt something when he knows and understands things with his mind. However, biblically speaking, that is not enough. Someone has only learnt something when he believes it in his heart and puts it habitually into practice.

You learn not just by hearing information, but by interacting with a mentor who explains theoretically what to do and shows you practically how to do it by doing it himself. Once you have made a habit of that practice, then you have learnt something.

An example of this difference is illustrated by the following anecdote: A certain church member approached a guest speaker after a service and said to him, 'I really liked your message; I learnt a lot from it'. The guest speaker answered, 'Sir, I am sorry to say, but you have only heard a lot. What you have learnt depends on what you do with what you have heard'.

Relationships

The biblical approach to learning is similar to the eastern style. It is more geared to the heart than to the mind; more focused on the practical than on the theoretical; more out of relationship than about simply receiving instruction. Although our culture is not used to this kind of education, it is still the most effective way of learning. That is why fathers or mentors are needed. The Church is crying out for fathers who are willing to invest themselves in others; fathers who take genuine interest in the lives of their spiritual children and who are willing to invest themselves in their development.

The development of the student is intensified when the relationships grows between the mentor and the student or between the father and the spiritual child. The extent to which the relationship grows and the student matures is directly related to the extent to which the mentor is prepared to devote himself to the task, to make all that he knows, and all that he has, available to the one whom he is mentoring, with no other motive than the development of the student. The mentor gives his love, respect and care freely. Paul expressed this kind of fatherly love to the church in Corinth:

> *'Now for the third time I am ready to come to you. And I will not be burdensome to you; for I do not seek yours, but you. For the children ought not to lay up for the parents, but the parents for the children. And I will very gladly spend and be spent for your souls; though the more abundantly I love you, the less I am loved.'* (2 Corinthians 12:14-15, NKJV)

Jesus is the greatest example of fathering. He preached to the multitudes, but He also took 12 disciples and taught and mentored them. He spent His life with them. He invested Himself in them. He gradually taught them what He knew and gave them the power He had. He showed them what it meant to be a genuine servant of God.

The disciples could see things functioning in the life of Jesus, so they started to ask questions. They learnt so much just by seeing Jesus living His life in service to the Father and by asking questions about His example. Jesus didn't teach them how to pray until they asked Him to. The disciples saw prayer functioning in Jesus' life and the impact it had and it made them ask Jesus to teach them how to pray. This is how they matured and were prepared for the tasks God had for them.

When Jesus finally gave them the Holy Spirit, He gave them all He knew and all He had (John 16:13; Acts 1:8). Jesus' desire was that they would do the same works He had done and even greater things (John 14:12-14). A true father is not threatened by his child when the child has the potential to become a greater success than himself – instead, he is excited. After three-and-a-half years together with Jesus, the disciples were ready to do the work for which He had called and trained them.

Principles for developing people

In order for the mentor or the father to develop his student or spiritual child, there are certain principles he must take into consideration. Speaking on parenting in his series *Raising Your Kids Without Raising Your Blood Pressure*, Rick Warren mentions five principles that will help the mentor to bring the best out of his student: accept their uniqueness; express their value; give them responsibility; bring correction; and love them unconditionally.

Accept the uniqueness of the student

Although the student is copying his or her mentor and in many ways will become like him, he or she will, at the same time, remain unique. The reason for this is simple: God has created each and every one of us differently. We are different in so many ways. We do not have the same strengths or weaknesses. We do not have the same temperaments. We do not have the same gifts, capacities or interests. That is why you cannot expect the same from everybody in every situation.

It is the mentor's job to help his students discover and become the people whom God made them to be. In fact, the mentor is to help the students to realise their uniqueness. This will set them free from trying to be someone they were never meant to be. It will also help the students to stop comparing themselves to others and to avoid conforming to what everybody else has become and is doing.

As everybody is unique, the mentor should know when to expect the student to conform and when to leave room for personal differences. This is certainly not easy and the mentor needs God's wisdom to get it right.

If the mentor expects the student to change in areas where he or she was not meant to change, then the mentor can hinder or even damage the student's growth and development instead of being a catalyst for good. God's general principles and purposes are the same for all of us, but the way they're expressed can differ from person to person.

Express the value of the student

One of the emotional needs that each person has is the knowledge that they are loved, that they are valued even though they are not perfect, and that there is someone who believes in them.

A father plays a big part in this. He must let his child know that he loves them. He does this by telling them and showing it in practical ways. One of the most important things a mentor can do is to show his love by giving his student his attention and his time.

Unfortunately, it is the time factor that is often the major hindrance. Developing true relationships takes time. If a mentor and student really want their relationship to be effective, they need to make quality time available in order to invest together. This may mean that they have to say 'no' to other activities that keep them from investing in their relationship. When the mentor and student do not take quality time to develop the father and son relationship, then there is no mentoring going on.

Give responsibility to the student

Nothing brings the best out of a person like giving them responsibility. People tend to become what they are expected to be. By giving the student responsibility, the mentor gives the student a sense that someone believes in him or her.

The only way to give someone responsibility is by giving them opportunities. The only way that people can become leaders is by leading. They can succeed or they can fail, but either way, it is part of the maturing process. They need to experience the fulfillment of success and the humility of failure in order to grow.

Just because there is the possibility of failure, the mentor should not deny his student the opportunity of trying. When the mentor tries to protect the student from failure, he turns them into a failure.

By giving the student opportunities, the mentor gives up a measure of his control and passes it to the student. The more mature the student becomes, the more control can be given to him or her (although the mentor should not give up too much control too soon!). The purpose of giving the student responsibility is not only to teach the student how to control his or her life and calling, but more importantly, how to live and minister under God's control and authority.

Bring correction to the student

Correction is an important part of fathering. Everyone needs correction from time-to-time because, like we said earlier, nobody is perfect. In the book of Proverbs, the importance of correction is frequently mentioned. Unfortunately, in our culture, the word 'correction' has gained a negative connotation. Part of the reason for this is the manner in which correction has been handled. It has damaged people instead of improving them. It is no accident that Paul warned natural fathers not to be the cause of the embittering of their children (Ephesians 6:4).

Done in the right way, correction is a great tool to help the student improve and grow. Actually, the Bible says that if we love our children we should correct them when it is needed: '*If you love your children, you will correct them; if you don't love them, you won't correct them*' (Proverbs 13:24, CEV).

The motive for correction must be love. The mentor corrects because it is in the interest of the student, not because it makes him feel good. Correction is not an end in itself, but a means to an end. It is to help the student grow and mature; it is to make the student better. The mentor has the best in mind for his student, so he is willing to bring correction. He would rather risk his relationship with the student by bringing correction than sit and watch them go in the wrong direction.

For correction to make the student better and not bitter, certain things need to be taken into consideration. For example, the language used will influence whether or not the correction will help the student to learn and to grow. Correction should also be done in a calm manner (Proverbs 29:11). Another key is that the mentor does not wait too long, especially if the matter is something the student has said or done. Lastly, although correction is required, the mentor should not correct too often and for every little detail. If a student is corrected on every minor thing, he or she will lose heart and want to give up: '*Parents, don't be hard on your children. If you are, they might give up*' (Colossians 3:21, CEV).

Love the student unconditionally

In the same way that God loves His children, a spiritual father should love his spiritual children. God loves His children unconditionally. This kind of love is expressed, for example, by giving forgiveness when forgiveness is needed. It is also expressed by never giving up on the person to whom he is a spiritual father.

There is nothing that we can do that will make God love us more. There is also nothing that we can do that will make God love us less. That is the same way a spiritual father should love his spiritual child. He must be willing to give his spiritual child a second chance, a third chance, a fourth chance and so on. Of course, true repentance on the part of the student is needed for the relationship to be restored.

Children – including spiritual children – can cause pain and disappointment to their parents. Parenting and mentoring can be frustrating, but love can conquer all things and always hopes for the best, even in the face of the biggest disappointments and mistakes: '*Love is always supportive, loyal, hopeful, and trusting*' (1 Corinthians 13:7, CEV).

Conclusion

There are people who call themselves apostles or spiritual fathers simply because they like the title, or because it makes them look important. That does not mean they are apostles or function as such. Those who call themselves 'apostle' or 'spiritual father' have often not built anything and do not carry the heart of a father. The only interest they have is not in those whom they are 'fathering', but in themselves.

True fathers and true mentors are very much needed in order to raise up the next generation; fathers who reflect the heart of God. Let's aim to become not only teachers to our people, but fathers and mothers in Israel: '*...villagers couldn't work in their fields. Then Deborah took command, protecting Israel as a mother protects her children*' (Judges 5:7, CEV).

Chapter 5
Apostles and the Local Church
Anthony Tselentakis

In Ephesians 4:1-14, we see the Apostle Paul talking about the Church, the Bride of Christ, and the things that God is doing to get her ready to meet Him. The Lord Himself is revealing to His believers the need for strong and healthy churches.

I have been saved for over 30 years and I have come to the conclusion that a healthy local church is vitally important for me and my family. I have seen lives and families fall apart because people have neglected their personal relationship with Christ, but also have neglected abiding and growing in a healthy local church where they can get proper nourishment, support and have good spiritual relationships. I have also seen many lives seriously hurt because the churches they were attending were not healthy, but strife and contention were in their midst.

The Apostle Paul writes in his epistles about the importance of being like-minded, having the same love, being of one accord and being of one spirit (Philippians 1:27; 2:2; Ephesians 4:1-6).

Pride, anger, judgment, bitterness and contentions are destroying lives and churches. Paul is beseeching the Body of Christ to have a spirit of lowliness, gentleness, meekness, longsuffering and to keep the unity of the Spirit in the bond of peace (Ephesians 4:1-3).

In the Sermon on the Mount, Jesus said: '*Blessed are the meek, for they shall inherit the earth*' (Matthew 5:5); '*Blessed are the merciful, for they shall obtain mercy*' (Matthew 5:7) and '*Blessed are the peacemakers, for they shall be called the sons of God*' (Matthew 5:9). The Apostle James said: '*For where envy and self seeking exist, confusion and every evil thing will be there*' (James 3:16).

Rebellion exists in our youth today because of strife and fighting in their homes. Contention and arguing creates an unhealthy environment for a child to grow properly. The same applies in some churches today. People are looking for a spiritual home where love and peace exist so their soul will find rest.

The Holy Trinity works in perfect harmony, order and peace. There is tremendous power where faith, love and peace exist because that is where the Holy Spirit will move, change and touch lives. When Christ ascended into heaven, at the right hand of the Father, He sent us the Holy Spirit to abide with, guide, and lead us (John 14-17). He encouraged them to have faith in Him; He told them about their access to the Father through His name. He taught a life of obedience to His commandments, abiding in His Word and the importance of the Holy Spirit in their lives. After He was resurrected, He breathed on them and said, '*Receive the Holy Spirit*' (John 20:22). He knew that only through the Holy Spirit would they be able to do what He had taught them. He knew that only with the Holy Spirit in their lives would they be effective in the ministry God called them to.

It is very important that we understand the ministry of the Holy Spirit in our lives and in our churches. It is He who moves in our midst and it is He who delegates as He wills (1 Corinthians 12:11). Jesus, through the Holy Spirit, gives different talents and gifts (Matthew 25:14-30). The reason He gives those talents is for the equipping of the saints for the work of ministry, *for the edifying of the body of Christ, His Church* (Ephesians 4:11-12).

Jesus is coming back to receive His Church and He wants her prepared as a bride adorned for her husband. The Lord gives these talents, gifts, activities and ministries (Ephesians 4; 1 Corinthians 12) to prepare and protect the bride. So if Jesus Himself gave some to be apostles, some prophets, some evangelists, and some pastors and teachers, that means we need apostles, prophets, evangelists, pastors and teachers. The fact that there are false ministers out there doesn't annul the fact that we need genuine Holy Ghost filled ministers for the edification of His Body.

The apostolic ministry was, and still is today, very important in the life of the Church. It is the ministry that will help establish local churches; it will father and nurture them in their first steps, and teach, equip and mentor leaders to lead these local churches.

Today, many people have heard the gospel of Jesus Christ and have accepted Jesus Christ as their Saviour, but are not rooted in a healthy church and later in life fall away. The great commission of Jesus Christ is to go and preach the gospel, see people saved and turn them into disciples. It is very important to go and preach the gospel to the lost, but it is also very important to nurture these spiritual infants and knit them into proper and healthy churches. I believe that for establishing good and healthy churches today there is a great need for good apostolic ministry. When Paul wrote to the church in Corinth (1 Corinthians 3) he warned them about the spirit of strife, but also about the way they built. Good intentions are not enough for building a good church. I have seen people who have been truly touched by God, being eager to serve Him with a pure motive, yet fail to build properly because of a lack of understanding and ability. I have also seen people with very good intentions not fulfilling their calling because they were in a position they were never meant to be in. Let me illustrate what I am trying to say:

A construction worker has a toolbox full of tools. All tools are needed, yet there is a specific task for which each tool was made. A hammer is needed to nail things and not to be used as a screwdriver. There are different types and sizes of screwdrivers, wrenches and keys. The same applies in church. I have seen people strive to be something they were not made for: People who want to be in the choir yet do not have the proper voices; people who want to teach Sunday school yet don't have the calling of God to do so, yet they think that's the place for them.

While it is the pastor's responsibility to delegate and organise such ministries, when it comes to church leadership things are not that simple. I have seen people want to be pastors and yet were never meant to be pastors. I have seen people want to be evangelists or teachers yet they won't accept the fact that God has not called them into those positions. That is where the apostolic and prophetic ministries are needed. Experienced, seasoned and recognised apostles and prophets can confirm and help in the structure of a local church. I also believe that in the setting of elders in a local church, both the apostolic and prophetic ministries are needed because through the setting in of the right team the church will be able to thrive.

The Apostle Paul advised Timothy and Titus, who were travelling with him and learned from him, how to go about setting elders in new churches that he had started and established. He told them to look for proven character, not novices, having the ability to teach and of course having the right spirit and lifestyle. Being placed in the wrong position can make someone very frustrated, as well as those around them.

Another illustration is that of a football team. There are offensive players, midfielders, defenders and of course the goalkeeper. These players do not become professionals overnight. Through the years as they grow up, they are trained and their abilities and skills are revealed. Naturally, the coaches have a tremendous responsibility in spotting these gifts and skills and helping the players reach their full potential. Everyone wants to score and be the centre of attraction, yet that is not what makes a good team. You need the right players in all the positions to make a team successful.

The same applies to churches. All members are needed, yet they need to function in the role which they are best suited for. In 1 Corinthians 12:11, Paul writes to the Corinthians that when it comes to ministry gifts it is the *Holy Spirit* that distributes as *He wills*. Again, I believe that the Holy Spirit reveals and confirms through the anointed apostles and prophets the gifts that are given to people. The apostolic ministry is very important for the setting and confirmation of leadership in the local churches.

In the years I have been in the faith I have witnessed people with great gifting not fulfilling the call of God upon their lives because they wanted to be something they were not. There was a person I knew who had a tremendous evangelistic gift. He would talk to people and they would get saved and he would bring them to church like nobody else. That person would go to hospitals and people would get healed, receive Christ as their Lord and the Kingdom of God would expand. When that person saw that the church was growing because of his evangelistic gifting, he desired to become the pastor. He started a church, but that church never grew. The reason was that he wanted to function outside of God's calling. That is where I believe the apostolic ministry is greatly needed. There is a great need for experienced, seasoned, proven, fathering ministries who will help guide lives of ministers and churches.

Relationships at the leadership level are also very important. I can say for myself that it can be very lonely at the top. When I say 'top' I don't mean from a position of recognition or ruling over people, but within the context of responsibility. While a local pastor, with the elders, is called to serve the people, they are also called to make decisions that will affect the lives of people and the future of the church. In making these decisions it is very important to hear from God, but it is impossible not to make mistakes. Prayer is one of the most important keys in the Kingdom of God, and it should be part of the daily life of every Christian, much more the ministers of the gospel. It is in the prayer closet that the Lord will speak to His people, as also in the corporate gathering.

A lot of times we fail in our tasks because we don't wait to hear the Lord's direction. Jesus Himself is the perfect example of how we should pray, and He taught His disciples how to do it. Praying, though, is not enough for leading a church; otherwise the Lord Himself would not give some to be apostles, prophets, evangelists, pastors and teachers (Ephesians 4:11). On a leadership level, it is not enough to have help only from the local church. It is evident in the book of Acts and the epistles of Paul, Peter, James, and John that a church can go astray if it is not careful. Again, there is a need for seasoned, proven experienced ministers that will help in such cases. It is through relationships at a leadership level that leaders get stronger, wiser and more effective in the calling that God has given them. As I have said previously, I will not allow just anyone to give me advice on very important issues. I will listen to what people have to say, but I will pay much closer attention to someone that knows what he is talking about.

Theoretical knowledge and experience are different things. Certain ministers think that all they need is a set of books and that studying them will help them become better in what they have been called to. I love reading books, and I am very careful who writes those books and what they have accomplished in life. Although my knowledge will increase, the writers of these books don't know me personally, they don't know my family, my strengths, my weaknesses, my friends, the local church I am leading, the people that are helping me lead the local church, their families, the country I live in, the city I live in or the conditions of the country I live in.

For example, how many pastors have tried to put into practice the G12 Vision that worked in Colombia yet it was never meant for their particular city or their country. They did the same things, the same concept, the same procedures yet they never prospered. The reason is that God never called them to do something like the brothers in Latin America.

Again, how many people tried to build a church like David Yonggi Cho in South Korea and were shipwrecked? Was it a lack of faith, or love or loyalty to God? I believe not. While we can claim by faith our healing, our finances (applying the laws of God) and the salvation of our loved ones, we cannot claim the calling to a specific ministry by faith. *It is the Spirit that gives as He wills!* The writers of these books do not know you personally, nor the ministry or gifting that God has placed in your life. They do not know your temperament or your character. Proper apostolic ministry will save people from shipwreck! Having good, healthy relationships with fathering ministers helps people go through the storms of leadership life successfully.

Going back to my personal life, I will not allow random people to speak into my life on major issues. I want to talk with someone whom I can identify with and who will understand me. Respect is a major key when it comes to receiving advice from someone. Jesus, the Son of God who had the Spirit without measure (John 3), could not minister where He was not accepted and respected.

Furthermore, when choosing a mentor, one should look at their character and what they have accomplished throughout their life. That is why I believe young ministers cannot operate in the office of an apostle. There are so many things that a church leader will need to listen to from experienced pastors. I love and respect older ministers and love to hear their experiences, their successes and their failures. It is foolish not to listen to someone more experienced than you and go through heartache and pain because you do not want to listen but choose to learn the hard way.

Practical advice is very important, as is the judging of personalities. I personally believe that I know my Bible quite well, yet it is the practical things that I am still lacking in. I need to hear from someone who has gone through the same steps and has proven that he knows what he is talking about. Ministers who never started from scratch cannot advise me because they never went through what I went through. Pastors who have taken over big churches and made them bigger and very successful, who started being a lay-pastor with (maybe) ten people, cannot advise me how to build. They can help other ministers and churches who are going through similar situations. The reason I am writing this is not to belittle someone's apostolic ministry but to clarify that all apostolic ministries are not the same. Peter was called to the Jew, while Paul was called to the Gentile. Both had the signs of an apostle, but the Lord directed them in different paths.

How much authority then can an apostle have over a church or a pastor? The answer is in Revelation 2-3.

The Apostle John, one of the twelve disciples of Jesus wrote to seven churches in the book of Revelation by the commandment of Jesus. He is approving the angel (leader) of the church in Ephesus for validating those who were apostles and those who were not; the

Lord commended him on how he persevered, had patience and had laboured and proved himself. At the same time, he warned him about his first love!

The responsibility of proving who is an apostle falls on the leader of the church. To the church in Pergamos, the responsibility for allowing the doctrine of Balaam and not allowing the doctrine of the Nicolaitans falls on the leader of the local church. To the church in Thyatira the responsibility that a woman Jezebel, who called herself a prophetess and taught wrong and immoral things, was laid on the leader of the local church. Pastors and elders cannot blame others for allowing wrong spiritual food and teaching in their churches. Pastors and elders cannot be people pleasers and allow anything that comes around to pass into their churches.

I believe one of the greatest responsibilities in the leadership of the local church is the clear, pure teaching of the gospel and the words of Jesus Christ. The high priest Eli (1 Samuel 1-4) allowed things that he should not have, and the result was that he and his sons and all of Israel paid heavy consequences for that. The Apostle John gave apostolic advice, correction and encouragement to the leaders of these seven churches. He saw things they didn't and couldn't, probably because of pressure from either church members or society itself. However, once apostolic input has been received, it is the leaders' responsibility to choose how they will respond to it. That is why I believe we need proper, healthy relationships with seasoned, proven, experienced apostolic ministers from whom we can receive the proper encouragement and correction in season.

The Apostle John again is writing to Gaius (3 John) and is encouraging him about his labour in the Lord. In that local church though there was someone, with the name of Diotrephes, who loved pre-eminence and would not receive the apostolic ministry of John. *Whose?* John's, one of the three closest to Jesus! The one whom Jesus told to take care of His mother! The one who saw Jesus on the mount of transfiguration! The one to whom Jesus revealed who would betray Him! The one with whom Jesus wanted to spend his final hours before His crucifixion praying in the garden of Gethsemane! Diotrephes was a person who liked authority and having a strong say-so in the local church he attended. He would not receive John or his fellow workers because of *pride*! He spoke against the original apostles, and not only that, he would try and influence other people not to receive them and keep them away. That is an unteachable, proud, ungodly spirit. A lot of problems existed in the first church with the original Apostles, and a lot of problems exist today as the second coming of Jesus Christ is approaching. There will always be people in our midst who have the Diotrephes spirit. People who only rely on their own intellect, spiritual opinion and never seek advice from true apostolic ministries; people who are too wise in their own eyes and love *pre-eminence*!

Paul wrote about the same issue to the church of the Corinthians (2 Corinthians 11-12). It was Paul who stayed in Corinth for 18 months and helped the church get established and grow, with much labour and travail yet these people, once they stood on their feet, neglected the parenting spirit of Paul and would pay attention to other so-called apostolic ministries. Paul, through his epistles, is explaining to the church in Corinth the signs of his genuine apostleship and the wrong motives of other people who tried to enter the church and cause confusion. Paul had close relationships with the Corinthians and though he was not there all the time his love for that local body was expressed and shown by his life and works for that city.

So, in which way should we receive and express our love to apostolic ministries who have influenced our lives and our churches?

One of the signs of the latter days is being ungrateful. There are people who help us in our lives in various situations. When Jesus healed the ten lepers only one came back to thank Him. Jesus' response was, '*Did I not heal ten? Where are the other nine?*' (Luke 17:17). Jesus likes a thankful spirit and a thankful attitude. When Jesus sent the Twelve and the seventy out he said, '*Whoever receives you, receives me!*' So receiving true, authentic, apostolic ministers who have laboured with the local body and have blessed the local body is pleasing Jesus Himself.

One way to show gratitude is hospitality. Opening your home to ministers brings great blessings into your house. Look what happened to the widow in Zarephath when she gave her last piece of bread to the prophet Elijah! In times of famine she didn't lack a thing because she blessed the man of God (1 Kings 17:8-15). Also, let us look at the life of the Shunammite woman who was serving Elisha, the man of God. She was barren but the Lord blessed her with a miracle and gave her a son (2 Kings 4). Look at the blessings that came upon people who served and ministered to Jesus and the Apostles. As a matter of fact, Jesus condemned those places that would not receive His messengers.

To the believers in Philippi, Paul was very thankful for the financial blessings that were given to him. Believers today like to quote Philippians 4:19: '*And my God shall supply all your need according to His riches in glory by Christ Jesus*'. God is a provider of everything we have, but all the previous verses talk about the giving spirit of the Philippians to Paul and his apostolic ministry. Again, Paul had a close relationship with the church in Philippi and that's why he could talk to them in that way. God will truly bless our lives and our churches when we are thankful, hospitable and liberally give to true ministries like these.

I am writing all these things so we can understand that the apostolic ministry was not only for the first Church. Today, many churches believe that all they need is a local pastor and an eldership team or a board. I strongly believe that true, anointed apostolic ministry is needed for building healthier and stronger churches.

Chapter 6
Sons and Fathers
Apostles as Fathering Servants
Chip Kawalsingh

Much has already been said about what makes a true apostle; this chapter will focus on what makes a true son. Apostles are, by definition, relational and personal. Like a son with his own natural father, so should it be within a healthy spiritual father-son relationship. This relationship should be based on a friendship with a spiritual father who is not interfering or rude, nor abusive or lording, but who is loving and helpful, bringing guidance and wisdom as needed. This has to be a personal, one-to-one relationship.

There are many examples of this type of relationship in the Bible. For example: Moses was a spiritual father to Joshua, and Joshua was his spiritual son; Elijah was a spiritual father to Elisha, and Elisha was his spiritual son; Elisha himself was a spiritual father to over 100 men and they were spiritual sons to him; Samuel was a spiritual father to King David, and David was a spiritual son to him; Jesus was a spiritual father to twelve men – the twelve disciples – and they were his apprentices or spiritual sons; and the Apostle Paul was a spiritual father to many men, including Timothy (1 Timothy 1:2) and Titus (Titus 1:4). They were his 'true sons', even though they were not physically related to him. They were his spiritual sons and He was their caring mentor. Please note that it is not enough to have a spiritual father – you must take on the role of a son in order for it to be of any benefit to you.

I would like to focus on a single great example of a spiritual son and father in the Bible: Elijah and Elisha.

Elijah's call

> *'So Elijah went and found Elisha son of Shaphat ploughing a field. There were twelve teams of oxen in the field, and Elisha was ploughing with the twelfth team. Elijah went over to him and threw his cloak across his shoulders and then walked away. Elisha left the oxen standing there, ran after Elijah, and said to him, "First let me go and kiss my father and mother good-bye, and then I will go with you!" Elijah replied, "Go on back, but think about what I have done to you." So Elisha returned to his oxen and slaughtered them. He used the wood from the plough to build a fire to roast their flesh. He passed around the meat to the townspeople, and they all ate. Then he went with Elijah as his assistant.'* (1 Kings 19:19-21)

This scripture gives a clear and concise summary of Elisha's character and his attitudes. He was a hard worker and a team player ('*Elisha was ploughing with the twelfth team*'), and was submissive to his earthly parents. Elijah's call was an urgent one, yet it took Elisha some time to fully respond and follow him. Elijah, as a spiritual father, had to be understanding about Elisha's responsibilities and commitment to his earthly family. He gave Elisha time to decide what he was going to do. Elisha, the son, understood God's calling and knew what was required of him, which is why he responded in the way he did: '*First let me go kiss my father and mother good-bye, then I will go with you!*' He knew that his relationship with his earthy parents was about to change and that he needed to manage that change in the right way.

It is also clear that in that single moment, Elisha had decided to follow Elijah for life. He destroyed his earthly inheritance as he knew that he had been called to something more. Elisha resolved that there was no going back.

This attitude can also be seen in the lives of the disciples who, when called by Jesus, left their nets and followed Him:

> *'As Jesus was walking beside the Sea of Galilee, he saw two brothers, Simon called Peter and his brother Andrew. They were casting a net into the lake, for they were fishermen. "Come, follow me," Jesus said, "and I will send you out to fish for people." At once they left their nets and followed him.'* (Matthew 4:18-20, NIV)

The Apostle Peter, in particular, walked away from the greatest catch of his life, without hesitation:

> *'One day as Jesus was standing by the Lake of Gennesaret, the people were crowding around him and listening to the word of God. He saw at the water's edge two boats, left there by the fishermen, who were washing their nets. He got into one of the boats, the one belonging to Simon, and asked him to put out a little from shore. Then he sat down and taught the people from the boat.*
>
> *When he had finished speaking, he said to Simon, "Put out into deep water, and let down the nets for a catch."*
>
> *Simon answered, "Master, we've worked hard all night and haven't caught anything. But because you say so, I will let down the nets."*
>
> *When they had done so, they caught such a large number of fish that their nets began to break. So they signaled their partners in the other boat to come and help them, and they came and filled both boats so full that they began to sink.*
>
> *When Simon Peter saw this, he fell at Jesus' knees and said, "Go away from me, Lord; I am a sinful man!" For he and all his companions were astonished at the catch of fish they had taken, and so were James and John, the sons of Zebedee, Simon's partner. Then Jesus said to Simon, "Don't be afraid; from now on you will fish for people." So they pulled their boats up on shore, left everything and followed him.'* (Luke 5:1-11, NIV)

In John 6:60, we read that many of His disciples deserted Jesus because they found what He was asking of them too hard to follow.

Jesus turned to the Twelve and asked, '*Are you going to leave as well?*' Then Peter, the simple fisherman who left the catch of a lifetime to follow Jesus, said these incredible, covenant-making words: '*Lord, to whom would we go?*' Notice that he used the word 'whom', and not 'where'. Peter understood the need to devote himself to someone; a father who could help to lead and guide his life.

It's important to note that once Elisha decided to follow Elijah, he entered a season of service and observation. He was not leading meetings or being asked to do anything 'up front'; he was simply serving his spiritual father (2 Kings 3:11). Most Bible scholars agree that this season lasted between 11-13 years, during which Elijah would have been passing down wisdom and experience that would later help Elisha receive a true revelation of sonship.

Elisha's testing

> *'When the LORD was about to take Elijah up to heaven in a whirlwind, Elijah and Elisha were travelling from Gilgal. And Elijah said to Elisha, "Stay here, for the LORD has told me to go to Bethel." But Elisha replied, "As surely as the LORD lives and you yourself live,* ***I will never leave you!****" So they went down together to Bethel. The group of prophets from Bethel came to Elisha and asked him, "Did you know that the LORD is going to take your master away from you today?" "Of course I know," Elisha answered. "But be quiet about it." Then Elijah said to Elisha, "Stay here, for the LORD has told me to go to Jericho." But Elisha replied again, "As surely as the LORD lives and you yourself live,* ***I will never leave you.****" So they went on together to Jericho.*
>
> *'Then the group of prophets from Jericho came to Elisha and asked him, "Did you know that the LORD is going to take your master away from you today?" "Of course I know," Elisha answered. "But be quiet about it." Then Elijah said to Elisha, "Stay here, for the LORD has told me to go to the Jordan River." But again Elisha replied, "As surely as the LORD lives and you yourself live,* ***I will never leave you.****" So they went on together.*
>
> *'Fifty men from the group of prophets also went and watched from a distance as Elijah and Elisha stopped beside the Jordan*

> *River. Then Elijah folded his cloak together and struck the water with it. The river divided, and the two of them went across on dry ground! When they came to the other side, Elijah said to Elisha,* ***"Tell me what I can do for you before I am taken away."*** *And Elisha replied,* ***"Please let me inherit a double share of your spirit and become your successor."*** *"You have asked a difficult thing," Elijah replied.* ***"If you see me*** *when I am taken from you, then you will get your request. But if not, then you won't."*
>
> *'As they were walking along and talking, suddenly a chariot of fire appeared, drawn by horses of fire. It drove between the two men, separating them, and Elijah was carried by a whirlwind into heaven. Elisha saw it and cried out,* ***"My father! My father!*** *I see the chariots and charioteers of Israel!" And as they disappeared from sight, Elisha tore his clothes in distress.*
>
> *'Elisha picked up Elijah's cloak, which had fallen when he was taken up. Then Elisha returned to the bank of the Jordan River. He struck the water with Elijah's cloak and cried out, "Where is the LORD, the God of Elijah?" Then the river divided, and Elisha went across.*
>
> *'When the group of prophets from Jericho saw from a distance what happened, they exclaimed,* ***"Elijah's spirit rests upon Elisha!"*** *And they went to meet him and bowed to the ground before him.'*
> (2 Kings 2:1-15, NLT – note author's emphasis)

In this passage we read about the final days of Elijah's ministry. It is easy to see from this scripture that the long walk which Elijah and Elisha shared was truly a test. We can learn several principles from this amazing passage.

Firstly, it shows that your loyalty will be tested. They walked from Gilgal through to Jericho – a long journey on foot! – and Elijah gave Elisha many opportunities to turn around and leave. Elisha, however, was committed to serve Elijah right to the end. Three times Elisha said to Elijah *'I will never leave you!'* Such was their relationship, the son wanted to stay with the father and refused to leave him.

The passage also demonstrates the principle of dedication. Elijah and Elisha walked together and spent time together: It takes a sacrifice of time from both the father and the son to develop a true relationship.

Without the dedication of both parties to the relationship it is not possible to build anything long-term.

This journey (the whole time they were together, not just the final walk) in Elisha's life was a lesson. He was being prepared for the work that God wanted him to do in the future. The key to learning the lesson was spending time serving and observing Elijah. A son must spend real time with his father to learn from his wisdom and example.

Perhaps the key lesson from this scripture is found in their shared happiness to just be together: Their relationship started out as that of a master and his servant, but by the end Elisha was only concerned with doing what God had for him. It didn't matter to Elisha what he got out of it personally. As Dick Iverson says, 'It does not matter the part you play as much as what you are a part of'. This passage clearly shows the importance of covenant love over convenient love. Elisha had dedicated himself to Elijah and refused to back out of that covenant for anything. Elisha's role was that of a servant, but his heart was that of a son.

God's timing

At just the right time, Elijah asked the right question and Elisha gave just the right answer: '*When they came to the other side, Elijah said to Elisha, "Tell me what I can do for you before I am taken away." And Elisha replied, "Please let me inherit a double share of your spirit and become your successor"*' (2 Kings 2:9). Elisha knew that time was running out and that Elijah would soon be gone, but notice that he never asked for a thing. It was Elijah who asked the question.

This prompted Elijah's reply: '*"You have asked a difficult thing," Elijah replied. "If you see me when I am taken from you, then you will get your request. But if not, then you won't"*' (2 Kings 2:10). Why was it difficult? It was difficult because the double portion was an honour reserved for the father's firstborn son, and would not have been given to a servant. Elijah's words have more to them than first meets the eye. He replied '*if you see me...*', but it could be read as 'how you see me...'.

> '*Elisha saw it and cried out, "My father! My father! I see the chariots and charioteers of Israel!" And as they disappeared from sight, Elisha tore his clothes in distress.*' (2 Kings 2:12)

Look at those words. Elisha's perception of Elijah had changed; he was no longer 'Master' but 'Father'. This revelation transformed him into a son, and so the rights of the firstborn could then be granted. Elisha received a double portion of Elijah's spirit. Elisha picked up Elijah's spirit and understood what was needed from him for a successful ministry. The double portion was not just symbolic, but real: Elisha performed twice as many miracles as Elijah did and his ministry lasted longer.

The group of prophets only saw Elijah as a master (2 Kings 2:3, 5), but it was only when Elisha saw him as a father that he received the mantle (2 Kings 2:12). Servants carry their master's burdens, but sons carry a greater level of anointing, and it's their responsibility to continue the father's work and to raise up sons themselves.

Father's function

Spiritual fathers are essential to the smooth functioning of the local church. By imparting their experience to their sons, they are able to gently steer the church away from danger. One of the key functions of a father is to bring a spirit of caution, to help steady the ship and prevent his sons from being blown about by the changing winds of popular teachings. Paul writes: '*I am not writing these things to shame you, but to warn you as my beloved children*' (1 Corinthians 4:14). '*Warn*', in the Greek, is the word '*noutheteo*', meaning 'admonish', 'caution', 'exhort'. Paul is sharing his wisdom to keep the church in Corinth from danger. Paul writes again:

> '*And you know that we treated each of you as a father treats his own children. We pleaded with you, encouraged you, and urged you to live your lives in a way that God would consider worthy. For he called you to share in his Kingdom and glory.*' (1 Thessalonians 2:11-12)

He is reinforcing his role as a father to the church, showing them that he loves them as his own children and speaks into their lives as such. Note, again, that Paul pleads, encourages and urges – he does not order or impose his will. A loving father uses his relationship with his son to build, not control.

Possibly the greatest service that a spiritual father provides is to set a good example for his sons. Apostles are a living example of how God wants the church to grow and behave: '*So I urge and implore you, be imitators of me*' (1 Corinthians 4:16).

However, sometimes a passive example is not sufficient, and in those times it is the role of the father to bring adjustment and, if necessary, discipline; but it is always out of a spirit of love and through strong, honest relationships.

> '*But I will come to you [and] shortly, if the Lord is willing, and then I will perceive and understand not what the talk of these puffed up and arrogant spirits amount to, but their force (the moral power and excellence of soul they really possess). For the kingdom of God consists of and is based on not talk but power (moral power and excellence of soul). Now which do you prefer? Shall I come to you with a rod of correction, or with love and in a spirit of gentleness?*' (1 Corinthians 4:19-21, AMP)

The relationships between spiritual fathers and sons are an essential element of the local church. Without strong spiritual fathers, we cannot have strong spiritual sons and daughters. Again, scripture declares that the entire world is waiting for the '*manifestation of the sons of God*' (Romans 8:19). When those genuine relationships work as God intended, they provide accountability, direction and wisdom which lead to a healthy spiritual life, and it's on that foundation that everything else is built, including, amongst other things, better marriages, godly households and personal advancement.

Spiritual fathers are a blessing to their sons and help to ensure longevity of their ministry and double their effectiveness – one godly man is good, two are always better! When fathers succeed in passing their spirit to their sons, the sons begin to raise up their own spiritual sons and daughters. The relationships that they build serve to strengthen and uphold one another, and together they form an army of godly men and women who will stand shoulder-to-shoulder for Christ and who will, ultimately, witness the final victory when the Bride of Christ, the Church, will prevail and God's Kingdom is established on the earth.

Chapter 7

Titles and Towels

Gordon Tose

As Christians, we are called not just to believe in Christ, but to be like Christ. The Apostle Paul tells us: '*Rather, clothe yourselves with the Lord Jesus Christ*' (Romans 13:14, NIV). Indeed, Paul equates spiritual maturity, which is surely the goal of all Christians, with '*attaining to the whole measure of the fullness of Christ*' (Ephesians 4:13, NIV). In other words, we are to aspire to live this life demonstrating the perfectly balanced character of Christ. Of course, there are a number of different aspects to this and the one I want to focus on is Christ's characteristic of humility, which manifested itself in His willingness to serve.

> *'Your attitude should be the same as that of Christ Jesus: Who, being in very nature God, did not consider equality with God something to be grasped, but made himself nothing,* ***taking the very nature of a servant****, being made in human likeness. And being found in appearance as a man,* ***he humbled himself*** *and became obedient to death – even death on a cross!'* (Philippians 2:5-8, NIV)

Paul's assessment of Christ's ministry was no more than Jesus said of Himself: '*Just as the Son of Man did not come to be served,* ***but to serve****,* *and to give his life as a ransom for many*' (Matthew 20:28, NIV). As Christians, therefore, it is fundamentally important that our lives display this characteristic of Jesus; the truth of this being beautifully illustrated in the following scripture:

> *'It was just before the Passover Feast. Jesus knew that the time had come for him to leave this world and go to the Father. Having loved his own who were in the world, he now showed them the full extent of his love. (...) Jesus knew that the Father had put all things under his power, and that he had come from God and was returning to God; so he got up from the meal, took off his outer clothing, and wrapped a towel round his waist. After that, he poured water into a basin and began to wash his disciples' feet, drying them with the towel that was wrapped round him. (...) When he had finished washing their feet, he put on his clothes and returned to his place. "Do you understand what I have done for you?" he asked them. "You call me 'Teacher' and 'Lord', and rightly so, for that is what I am. Now that I, your Lord and Teacher, have washed your feet, you also should wash one another's feet.* ***I have set you an example that you should do as I have done for you.****"'* (John 13:1, 3-5, 12-15, NIV)

I find that absolutely amazing. Jesus, who '*knew that the Father had put all things under his power*', chose an act of humility, rather than an act of power, as the example His disciples should follow. What makes this act of service even more powerful is the realisation of just whose feet He washed. He washed the feet of Thomas who Jesus knew would doubt Him. He washed the feet of Peter who He knew would disown Him. And then, incredibly, He washed the feet of Judas who He knew would betray Him. The Christian way is most definitely not the way of self-service, and indeed is the exact opposite; it is the way of selfless service. '*If anyone would come after me*', Jesus said, '*he must deny himself and take up his cross* ***daily*** *and follow me*' (Luke 9:23, NIV). That word 'daily' emphasises that this selflessness is to be a lifestyle and not a few isolated acts of service in an otherwise self-centred existence. Jesus goes on to say: '*For whoever wants to save his life will lose it, but whoever loses his life for me will save it*' (Luke 9:24, NIV). What this suggests is that laying down what we want in favour of what Jesus wants leads to us gaining something of much greater value. This idea of loss leading to greater gain is found in all four Gospels, neither is it an isolated concept (see Matthew 10:37-39; 16:24-27; 19:29; Mark 8:34-37; 10:29-30; Luke 17:33; 18:29-30 and, in a slightly different form, John 12:25-26). No other principle laid down by Jesus is given such emphasis and, as such, it is something we need to pay particular attention to. Certainly this concept of selfless service is picked up by the Apostles:

> *'You, my brothers, were called to be free. But do not use your freedom to indulge the sinful nature; rather,* ***serve one another*** *in love.'* (Galatians 5:13, NIV)

> *'Each one should use whatever gift he has received* ***to serve others,*** *faithfully administering God's grace in its various forms.'* (1 Peter 4:10, NIV)

> *'Be shepherds of God's flock that is under your care,* ***serving as overseers*** *– not because you must, but because you are willing, as God wants you to be; not greedy for money,* ***but eager to serve;*** *not lording it over those entrusted to you, but being examples to the flock.'* (1 Peter 5:2-3, NIV)

Peter then goes on to write in verse 4, *'And when the Chief Shepherd appears, you will receive the crown of glory that will never fade away'*, which, of course, is a restating of the principle that those who lay down their own interests will inherit something of far more value.

What these two scriptures from 1 Peter also emphasise is that 'ministry' is given for the benefit of those who receive it, rather than for the benefit of those who exercise it. This poses a particular challenge to us all because it confronts something we all struggle with in one form or another, and that is pride. Pride is destructive.

> *'How you have fallen from heaven, O morning star, son of the dawn! You have been cast down to the earth, you who once laid low the nations! You said in your heart, "I will ascend to heaven; I will raise my throne above the stars of God; I will sit enthroned on the mount of assembly, on the utmost heights of the sacred mountain. I*

will ascend above the tops of the clouds; I will make myself like the Most High." But you are brought down to the grave, to the depths of the pit.' (Isaiah 14:12-15, NIV)

It is impossible for us to imagine Lucifer in his exalted position in Heaven prior to his fall from grace. Jesus Himself said in reference to this event: *'I saw Satan fall like lightning from heaven'* (Luke 10:18, NIV). It was pride that filled Lucifer's heart, and it proved to be his downfall.

'Pride goes before destruction, a haughty spirit before a fall.' (Proverbs 16:18, NIV)

Pride manifests itself in numerous ways. An unwillingness to take correction with the right attitude is one such manifestation, as is being possessive of our role (which I will examine in more detail further on in this chapter); as is selfish ambition - and every single one of us has the potential to be overcome by it. In my years at Huddersfield Christian Fellowship I have witnessed two men who enjoyed positions of real privilege in the church, but for them that was not enough; they wanted more. The outworking of their pride not only shipwrecked their own lives but also had devastating consequences for their families. They paid a high price for their pride and will one day have to give an account to the Lord who, the Bible says, 'detests all the proud of heart' (Proverbs 16:5). In essence, they succumbed to the same selfish ambition that led to Lucifer's loss of position. The Bible has some extremely strong words on this subject:

'The acts of the sinful nature are obvious: sexual immorality, impurity and debauchery; idolatry and witchcraft; hatred, discord, jealousy, fits of rage, ***selfish ambition****, dissensions, factions and envy; drunkenness, orgies, and the like. I warn you, as I did before, that those who live like this will not inherit the kingdom of God.'* (Galatians 5:19-21, NIV)

'Do nothing out of ***selfish ambition*** *or vain conceit, but in humility consider others better than yourselves. Each of you should look not only to your own interests, but also to the interests of others.'* (Philippians 2:3-4, NIV)

> *'Who is wise and understanding among you? Let him show it by his good life, by deeds done in the humility that comes from wisdom. But if you harbour bitter envy and* ***selfish ambition*** *in your hearts, do not boast about it or deny the truth. Such "wisdom" does not come down from heaven but is earthly, unspiritual, of the devil. For where you have envy and* ***selfish ambition****, there you find disorder and every evil practice.'* (James 3:13-16, NIV)

So we see from these scriptures that selfish ambition is spoken of in the same breath as witchcraft; is the very opposite of humility and has the devil himself as its source.

Is it any wonder that God is opposed to it? Is it any wonder that Korah in Numbers 16 suffered the fate he did? Korah was ambitious. He was not ambitious for the Kingdom of God, nor was he ambitious for the nation of Israel; he was ambitious for himself and his ambition caused him to gather people round him. Then, once he felt secure enough, he led his followers in opposing God's delegated authority. Korah made the mistake that many have made in that he assumed his self-appointment legitimised his opposition to those whom God had appointed. In reality, Korah already had important duties in the tabernacle, but he wanted more; he wanted to be a priest and his ambition put him in direct conflict, not with Moses and Aaron, but with God Himself. In fact the scripture tells us that the ambition of Korah and those who supported him was equivalent to treating '*the LORD with contempt*' (Numbers 16:30, NIV), and God destroyed every single one of them.

The two men I referred to earlier are still living, but it seems to me that what they could have had in God was destroyed just as comprehensively. Korah's fate is a warning to us all. As I stated earlier, we are all subject to the temptation of pride and as such need to heed Paul's words to the Corinthians: '*So, if you think you are standing firm, be careful that you don't fall!*' (1 Corinthians 10:12, NIV). It is an unfortunate truth that no church has been, or will be, free from those who have been overcome by the seductive power of pride.

> *'Keep watch over yourselves and all the flock of which the Holy Spirit has made you overseers. Be shepherds of the church of God, which he bought with his own blood. I know that after I leave, savage wolves will come in among you and will not spare the flock.* ***Even from your own number men will arise and distort the truth in order to draw away disciples after them.*** *So be on your guard!'* (Acts 20:28-31, NIV)

Korah distorted the truth when he accused Moses of leading the Israelites '*out of a land flowing with milk and honey*' (Numbers 16:13, NIV). Pride, it seems, has a peculiar way of interpreting the facts. But who is '*from your own number*'? Is it one from those who sit in the congregation? It certainly could be. However, it is more likely to be one from those who sit within the leadership team. Korah was part of the team, as was Lucifer. It seems that pride becomes a greater danger the more prominent a person becomes.

A servant's heart is the opposite of a proud heart. A servant's heart is what God exalts; a proud heart is what God opposes. Which heart we possess will determine our motives for doing the things we do. If our motives are in any way self-centred and driven by pride this can lead to us having a competitive nature, being preoccupied with status and having a disregard for integrity.

Having a competitive nature

Competition is very much part of the world in which we live and we are confronted by it from a relatively early age. School is basically a competition. In recent times the UK authorities have tried to remove the competitive element from schools and replace it with the illusion that nobody loses. However, the reality is that the students who get the best results tend to get the best university places which tend to lead to the best jobs. That sounds like a competition to me. Once in employment, we find ourselves competing with our fellow employees as we look to gain promotion. If we have our own business, we compete with all the other businesses in the same field as ourselves. In the world of nature, males compete for a mate and this applies equally in the world of humans. It would be reasonable to suggest, therefore, that it is part of our nature to be competitive; it is part of what we are. However, to let it have free rein as a Christian directly conflicts with the whole principle of serving, which is one of the foundation stones on which our faith is built.

How can a competitive nature be reconciled with Paul's instruction to be '*devoted to one another in brotherly love. Honour one another above yourselves*' (Romans 12:10, NIV)? How can we even think of competing with each other when we read: '*Therefore encourage one another and build each other up*' (1 Thessalonians 5:11, NIV)? Yes, as Christians, we have to operate in the fields of education, employment and business, but the Bible is very clear: '*Whatever you do, work at it with all your heart, as working for the Lord, not for men, since you know that you will receive an inheritance from the Lord as a reward. It is the Lord Christ you are serving*' (Colossians 3:23-24, NIV). It is as we adopt this instruction in every area of our lives that God grants us success, promotion and favour.

In 1 Samuel 18:14, we read of David: '*In everything he did he had great success, because the LORD was with him*' (NIV). We are to trust in the Lord and not in any natural abilities we may have in order to be better than others. People who are overly competitive have to win because winning is evidence of their value and importance. They have failed to recognise that their value and importance, in God's eyes, lie in who they are and not in what they achieve. In a church environment, a competitive nature leads at best to disharmony, and at worst to conflict.

Being preoccupied with status

People preoccupied with status love titles. They love titles because a title usually comes with influence and influence is what they seek. In order to achieve their ambition, they will involve themselves in all kinds of useful activities, but they will want to make sure they are seen doing them by all the right people. This is the very opposite of the heart of a servant who is happy to serve just for the sake of serving, content in the knowledge that, while nobody might see what they do, God sees. Those who strive for influence are very concerned about how they appear; not necessarily to those over whom they have influence, but certainly to those who can give them that influence.

They will make sure the pastor is aware of what they have done. They will support something the pastor is involved in, but will be reluctant to support anything a 'competitor' initiates. Nor will they be content to wait for recognition and they will not hesitate to ask for 'position' this request being evidence that their motivation is self-centred. To my mind, a good example of someone overly concerned with their title is Miriam.

> *'Miriam and Aaron began to talk against Moses because of his Cushite wife, for he had married a Cushite. "Has the LORD spoken only through Moses?" they asked. "Hasn't he also spoken through us?" And the LORD heard this.'* (Numbers 12:1-2, NIV)

It is important to note that, while it appears to have been Miriam and Aaron who confronted Moses, it was in fact Miriam who instigated the confrontation. The pretext was the nationality of Moses' wife, whereas the real problem was Miriam's perception of her position. In the previous chapter we are told of a very special meeting:

> *'So Moses went out and told the people what the LORD had said. He brought together seventy of their elders and made them stand round the Tent. Then the LORD came down in the cloud and spoke with him, and he took of the Spirit that was on him and put the Spirit on the seventy elders. When the Spirit rested on them, they prophesied, but they did not do so again.'* (Numbers 11:24-25, NIV)

All of a sudden, Miriam, in her eyes, is not so special anymore. There had been a change in her title. Instead of being 'the' prophet (or prophetess), she was now just 'a' prophet. She had been held in high regard by the Israelites, but now her prophetic role was no longer so unique. Now there were seventy others who were prophesying. How was she to know that they would not do so again? She had come to value her prophetic gift and the prominence that it gave her. This was where her security lay and, unable to overcome her sudden insecurity, she uses Moses' wife as a way of voicing her complaint. This is just another example of an incorrect motivation causing disharmony and conflict.

Having a disregard for integrity

The philosophy of those whose motives are prideful and self-centred can certainly include an element of 'the ends justify the means'. In other words, the goal is all-important and the journey is purely the means of reaching the destination. This is a dangerous philosophy because the Bible clearly demonstrates that God is very interested in the journeys we take and uses our journeys to shape us into the people He wants us to be. The problem with being overly focussed on the destination is that there is the temptation to make the journey as short as possible, which leads to taking shortcuts. Shortcuts, as a way of life, can only be justified if we lie to ourselves about our motives and convince ourselves that the end results are desirable; which indeed they may be. It is the motive that presents the problem, which is why being at peace with the motive is so vital.

A typical justification goes like this: Having been assured that the end result (the first element in the process) is desirable, all that remains is the conviction that the motive (the second element) is pure. Once this conviction is arrived at, then even if the means of obtaining the end result (the third element) is questionable, this can be accommodated because 'two out of three is not unreasonable' and the question of integrity can be avoided. This is clearly false. When a Christian displays such a lack of integrity, it not only has a negative effect on their own personal relationship with God, it can also have a negative effect on the non-believer's perception of God. *'As it is written: "God's name is blasphemed among the Gentiles because of you."'* (Romans 2:24, NIV).

What is common to all those who are proud of heart is that the goals they strive for are all external; goals that include greater reputation, prominence and influence. However, the way of pride is doomed to fail because *'a man's pride brings him low, but a man of lowly spirit gains honour'* (Proverbs 29:23, NIV). It is far better to be motivated by a love of service.

> *'After this, Jesus and his disciples went out into the Judean countryside, where he spent some time with them, and baptised. Now John also was baptising at Aenon near Salim, because there*

> *was plenty of water, and people were constantly coming to be baptised.* (...) *They* (John's disciples) *came to John and said to him, "Rabbi, that man who was with you on the other side of the Jordan – the one you testified about – well, he is baptising, and everyone is going to him". To this John replied, "A man can receive only what is given him from heaven. You yourselves can testify that I said, 'I am not the Christ but am sent ahead of him.' The bride belongs to the bridegroom. The friend who attends the bridegroom waits and listens for him, and is full of joy when he hears the bridegroom's voice. That joy is mine, and it is now complete. He must become greater; I must become less."'* (John 3:22-23, 26-30, NIV)

Those who love to serve understand the difference between ownership and stewardship. It is certainly true that John had a charisma that drew the crowd to him and it would be fair to say that his ministry was flourishing, but some of his followers delivered the news that everyone was now going to Jesus. Basically they were saying to John, 'If you don't do something about this, your ministry will be finished.' John's response to this news was, *'A man can receive only what is given him from heaven'*. He understood that the crowd was not his and that he was merely looking after it for a time. That time had now come to an end and John was at peace with that. I have seen too many examples over the years of people who were given a role as a steward, but who ended up trying to be its owner. When it was eventually taken away from them there was only heartache and distress.

Those who love to serve understand their identity. John knew who he was and he knew who he was not: *'You yourselves can testify that I said, "I am not the Christ but am sent ahead of him"'*. Despite his popularity, John did not see himself as the bridegroom and only ever saw himself as the bridegroom's 'best man'. This understanding of his true identity meant that when his popularity decreased, it did not affect his peace and his joy. Too many people, Christians included, derive their identity from the role they fulfil and when that role is no longer theirs, there is the potential for their life to be in crisis. Our identity should be who we are in relation to God, not what we are in relation to the church or any other organisation.

Those who love to serve understand their purpose; they know what they have been called to do. John's purpose was that of the 'best man' and nothing else. It was not his purpose to be the bridegroom. His role was to make sure everyone's attention was on the bridegroom and not on himself. He pointed to Christ. His role was to make sure he prepared the way for Jesus; that was his purpose. '*This is he who was spoken of through the prophet Isaiah: "A voice of one calling in the desert, 'Prepare the way for the Lord, make straight paths for him'"*' (Matthew 3:3, NIV). John had no wish to aspire to anything beyond what was his to do. He had no ambition other than an ambition to do what God had called him to do. A consistent prayer of mine has been, 'Lord, I only want to do what you want me to do; nothing more; nothing less.' What could possibly bring greater fulfilment than to be occupied with what God has for us?

Those who love to serve understand commitment. They understand commitment to a cause and they understand commitment to other people. '*He must become greater; I must become less*' (John 3:20, NIV). Those who are full of pride stay the course only as long as they get what they desire: more attention; more influence. John's popularity could have caused him to lessen his commitment to Jesus and focus on his own ministry, but because he stayed true to his calling, the outcome was a wonderful sense of joy.

> '*The bride belongs to the bridegroom. The friend who attends the bridegroom waits and listens for him, and is full of joy when he hears the bridegroom's voice. That joy is mine, and it is now complete.*' (John 3:29, NIV)

So, the question for us all is: Do we desire to be served or do we find joy in serving? The answer to that will point to whether we are proud or whether we are humble. How honest our answer is will depend on how deeply we have examined our motives. Why do we do the things we do?

These are the words of Paul to the church in Rome; words we would all do well to pay attention to: '*For by the grace given me I say to every one of you: Do not think of yourself more highly than you ought, but rather think of yourself with sober judgement, in accordance with the measure of faith God has given you*' (Romans 12:3, NIV).

What Paul is saying is that whatever gift we may feel we have; whatever ministry we operate in; the power to do so comes from God and as such there is no basis for a superior attitude. However, it is only by being prepared to be brutally honest with ourselves that we will be able to continually adjust our attitude to be '*that of Christ Jesus*'.

Chapter 8
Prophetic Teams
Form, Function and Fidelity
Chip Kawalsingh

As we have already read in previous chapters, New Testament prophets operate on a different level to that of their Old Testament counterparts. New Testament prophets - and indeed New Testament prophecy – fall into one of four categories: edification (to stir up); exaltation (to build up); comfort (to bind up) or conviction (to open up). In order to see how they should function together, we must look at 1 Corinthians 14.

> *'Let two or three people prophesy, and let the others evaluate what is said. But if someone is prophesying and another person receives a revelation from the Lord, the one who is speaking must stop. In this way, all who prophesy will have a turn to speak, one after the other, so that everyone will learn and be encouraged. Remember that people who prophesy are in control of their spirit and can take turns.'* (1 Corinthians 14:29-32, NLT)

It's important to note that this scripture describes an order and function as to how prophecy should be conducted. When prophets come together within a local church they should always submit to the pastor of that church – this is important! They are not there to take over authority or make demands, they are there simply to serve by edifying, exhorting and speaking words that comfort and bring forth conviction.

> *'Now these are the gifts Christ gave to the church: the apostles, the prophets, the evangelists, and the pastors and teachers.'* (Ephesians 4:11, NLT)

Notice that these abilities are just gifts which are given freely by Christ. They do not, in any way, serve to prove the holder's holiness or purity; they are just gifts! Notice, also, that these gifts are given to the Church. In other words, the local church is the ground in which these gifts are meant to be planted, nurtured and developed.

The fidelity of the prophetic word

One thing to understand about New Testament prophets is that they are not infallible. No New Testament prophet was ever used in the utterance of infallible scripture. Instead, most of the New Testament was written by the Apostles. All prophetic words must be judged in accordance with scripture.

In his book *Prophetic Gatherings in the Local Church*, Brain Daehn says 'no prophetic ministry, except Christ, was ever a perfect channel'. How, then, do we test prophetic words and the ministry of the prophet? Well, let's go back to the three sources of prophetic words: the Holy Spirit, the human spirit and the evil spirit.

It's important to note that the Holy Spirit is the only true source of prophecy: *'For prophecy never had its origin in the human will, but prophets, though human, spoke from God as they were carried along by the Holy Spirit'* (2 Peter 1:21, NIV).

When the Holy Spirit speaks to man, it's more in the form of an impression rather than actual writing on a wall or an audible voice. The impression is then left to the prophet to act upon. As this requires human involvement, there can be problems. The impression can be wrongly interpreted or the prophet may simply fail to recognise or act upon it. It's for this reason that any prophecy must be checked against scripture.

'Prophecy' is not limited to Holy Spirit inspiration. The human spirit is capable of – and indeed, inclined to – prophesy by itself. There's an alertness of spirit that occurs in prophetic gatherings that causes everyone to want to prophesy. Ezekiel 13 clearly talks about those who prophesy out of their own hearts, and we must be careful not to step out of the Spirit and walk in the flesh (Galatians 5:13-18).

Evil spirits are also responsible for some prophecy. This is demonstrated in scripture when Jesus asks Peter, '*Who do people say the Son of Man is?*' (Matthew 16:13). Peter replied '*You are Christ, Son of the Living God*'. Jesus affirms this by saying '*this was not revealed to you by flesh and blood, but by my Father in heaven*'. A few verses later, Jesus turned to Peter and said '*Get behind me Satan!*' in response to Peter's prophecy that His death and resurrection would not occur. It is clear from this passage that evil spirits are also capable of being the source of prophetic words.

It should be obvious by now that prophecy is not a perfect or complete gift. Paul puts it this way: '*Now our knowledge is partial and incomplete, and even the gift of prophecy reveals only part of the whole picture!*' (1 Corinthians 13:9, NLT). However, we should be careful not to underestimate the importance of prophecy. Paul goes on to say: '*Do not scoff at prophecies, but test everything that is said. Hold on to what is good*' (1 Thessalonians 5:20-21, NLT).

It is therefore necessary to test the fidelity of any prophetic words against the written Word. There are seven questions which you must ask in order to test a prophetic word and determine whether it is genuine, Holy Spirit inspired prophecy.

Firstly, does it line up with scripture? It's important that prophetic words are scripturally sound. In the same way as preaching, songs, prayer and doctrine must line up with scripture, so prophecy must fall in line. Whenever Jesus spoke prophetically it lined up not only with the written scripture, but the spirit of those scriptures too, and echoed exactly what the Father had said before (John 5:19; John 8:28).

Second, does it carry the spirit of the Bible? As well as being doctrinally sound, does it carry the spirit of the written Word? Many things that claim 'thus saith the Lord', or 'the Lord will say', can be done outside the spirit of the Word. It's important that this spirit is not violated (Romans 13:1-2).

Third, does it conform to the procedure and authority of scripture? Everything must be done in the correct order and under the right authority. Prophets are subject to the authority of the senior leadership of the local church, which is in accordance with scripture (1 Timothy 5:17; Ephesians 4:11-12).

Fourth, does it bring condemnation? The word of the Lord never condemns, it only convicts. It cuts to the heart and propels us to where God wants us to go without making us feel like we've been put down, criticised or punished (Romans 8:1; 2 Timothy 1:7).

Fifth, does it come to pass? Too many prophetic words are given without anyone ever asking 'Did it come to pass?' This is an important test, and prophecy must be adjusted wherever and whenever needed (1 Thessalonians 5:21).

Sixth, does it bear witness with your spirit? Although the prophetic word convicts, it must also bear witness within your spirit. Anything that is unclear or doesn't feel right to the receiver should be cleared up by the senior leadership of the house (Romans 8:16).

Finally, are others in agreement with the word? There should be a general agreement between the prophets, senior leaders and the church about what has been prophesied. However, things are not always clear or obvious at first to those who are listening and judging the word (1 Peter 3:8; Romans 12:16).

The Bible is clear in what it has to say about judging the prophetic word: '*Let two or three prophets speak, and let the others judge*' (1 Corinthians 14:29, NKJV). The word '*judge*' here is the Greek '*diakrino*' (Strong's G1223 and G2919), meaning 'to separate thoroughly', 'to withdraw from', 'to oppose', 'to hesitate' or 'to discriminate', by implication 'to decide'. It is a strong call to the judge to be truly discerning about what should and should not be accepted as prophecy. It is the role of the leadership of that local house – the pastors and elders – to judge any prophecy brought within the local church.

A final note about the fidelity of prophetic words: Even if you receive a prophetic word which passes all the above tests and is judged to be true by those in authority over your life, you should continue to live by the wisdom of the Bible and not base your choices on prophecy. God's word will come to pass at the prescribed time, but it is dependent on your obedience to His Word. Prophecy is always subservient to the Word; we should avoid elevating and chasing after it.

Prophetic teams and presbytery

Presbytery is a meeting in which a group of prophets join together to prophesy over chosen and prepared members of the congregation under the authority and supervision of the leadership of the local church. A presbytery should consist of a team of three prophets, one of whom should be a senior prophet charged with bringing direction and wisdom. This form is illustrated in the book of Acts.

> *'Then the apostles and elders together with the whole church in Jerusalem chose delegates, and they sent them to Antioch of Syria with Paul and Barnabas to report on this decision. The men chosen were two of the church leaders – Judas (also called Barsabbas) and Silas.'* (Acts 15:22, NLT)

> *'Then Judas and Silas, both being prophets, spoke at length to the believers, encouraging and strengthening their faith.'* (Acts 15:32, NLT)

Prophets who wish to function in a presbytery need to meet specific criteria. The word 'presbyter' (one who is part of a prophetic team ministering at a presbytery) comes from the Greek word '*presbuteros*', from which we get the English word 'elder' in the New Testament. In order to be a presbyter, a prophet must meet the qualifications for an elder as laid down in the Bible.

> *'This is a trustworthy saying: "If someone aspires to be an elder he desires an honourable position." So an elder must be a man whose life is above reproach. He must be faithful to his wife. He must exercise self-control, live wisely, and have a good reputation. He must enjoy having guests in his home, and he must be able to teach. He must not be a heavy drinker or be violent. He must be gentle, not quarrelsome, and not love money. He must manage his own*

family well, having children who respect and obey him. For if a man cannot manage his own household, how can he take care of God's church? An elder must not be a new believer, because he might become proud, and the devil would cause him to fall. Also, people outside the church must speak well of him so that he will not be disgraced and fall into the devil's trap.' (1 Timothy 3:1-7, NLT)

From this scripture we can discern the qualities and characteristics of a presbyter. He should be an elder in his local church (not a new convert or a novice, although allowance can be made for young prophets being trained) and have a good godly character, high moral standards and a sound grasp of doctrine. He should not be influenced by money and should be regularly flowing in the prophetic in his own local church. Please note, although all these qualifications begin 'he', it is possible to include female presbyters, perhaps the wife of one of the other prophets in the team.

Preparing for presbytery

It's important that the candidates preparing to go through presbytery get themselves ready before the Lord. This will require at least three-to-four days of prayer and fasting prior to the presbytery meeting. This can be continued through the duration of the meeting (if it is to span two or more days), although eating lightly to regain strength is fine.

During these meetings, it is vitally important that there is a flow of worship. This will allow the prophetic mantle to fall on the presbyters in the meeting place. The candidate (or couple if the candidates are married) will be brought out and presented to the prophets. Once the mantle is resting on the prophets, each one will, in turn, prophesy over the candidate. The worship band should follow the lead of the prophets as to when they play and when they should stop to allow the word of the Lord to come. Once each presbyter has prophesied over the candidate, they can be sent back into the congregation and the next candidate can be called.

What happens next?

It is essential that the words be recorded and given to the candidates so they can listen to them again later, without the distractions and emotions of the meeting. It's highly recommended that the candidate is asked to transcribe the audio, and a meeting should be arranged between them and their pastors or elders to examine the word together.

The local leadership should guide the candidate through the prophecy and help them to understand it. They should also make sure the candidate is aware of the two parts of any prophecy: what God said He would do, and what they need to do. This distinction should always be at the forefront of the candidates' minds. It is important to wait and let God bring about what He said would happen. He is never in a hurry and often it can take years before such words come to pass.

Prophecy in the local church

It is clear from the Bible that the New Testament prophet is a necessary part of the five-fold ministry and a gift from Christ to His Church. It is also clear that New Testament prophets are not the same as their Old Testament predecessors, and are intended for a different function. They are not infallible, and so their words must be tested and proved against the wisdom of God's unchanging Word. By combining in teams, prophets are able to work together to discern and confirm God's word for individuals, bringing security and accountability to the practice of personal prophecy within the local church.

Most importantly, team ministry allows New Testament prophets to fulfil their calling and responsibility to bring edification, exaltation, comfort and conviction to God's people through His chosen vehicle on the earth, the local church.

Chapter 9
Five-fold Ministry Functioning in the Local Church

Memos Sakellariou

The five-fold ministry is a subject which has been well studied and understood by the Body of Christ. We all know and appreciate what each ministry is and what it does in isolation. In this study, though, we will take a different approach and look at the five-fold ministry from a different viewpoint: its role and function in the local church.

The negative phenomena which have been seen in people calling themselves 'apostle' or 'prophet' and so on are well-known. In most cases, it involves arrogance and the abuse of their titles. I say 'title' and not 'calling' very deliberately because a true apostle would not act to repress, abuse or exploit anyone.

We have all seen many forms, demonstrations and uses of these ministries, and, to a large extent, they have caused pain, division, confusion and rebellion in the Church. This should not surprise us; the Apostle Paul prophesied that they would centuries ago (Acts 20:29-31). There are, however, many ministers who work with the heart and Spirit of Christ and bring blessing and increase to the body of Christ.

We know that our Lord used simple examples from nature and everyday life to show us great truths. For example: '*The Kingdom of heaven is like a man who sowed good seed in his field*' (Matthew 13:24-30, NKJV). '*For we are God's fellow workers, you are God's field, you are God's building*' (1 Corinthians 3:9, NKJV).

Every local church is a field, a field of God, and we know that the field will bear fruit according to the seed sown. Each time we preach and each time we minister, we sow seed into that field. In time, that seed will bear fruit - whether it is good seed bringing good fruit, or bad seed which will bring forth problematic fruit.

So the five-fold ministry, wherever it is used, should produce specific fruit. This fruit is defined in the Word of God itself, in Ephesians 4:11-16. In this passage of scripture we see the fundamental purpose of these ministries in the local church.

> '*And He Himself gave some to be apostles, some prophets, some evangelists and some pastors and teachers, for the equipping of the saints, for the work of ministry, for the edifying of the body of Christ, till we all come to the unity of the faith and the knowledge of the Son of God, to a perfect man, to the measure of the stature of the fullness of Christ.*' (Ephesians 4:11-13)

The first important phrase in this scripture is '*for the equipping*'. In Ancient Greek this is '*pros ton katartismon*'. The word '*katartismon*' comes from the verb '*kat–artizo*'. We only find this word in this one verse; it is not used anywhere else in the Bible. Its meaning is very important; you could even say unique: 'to bring to order'; 'to set in a straight direction'; 'to improve lives'; 'to make the saints perfect'.

With this meaning we can understand why the Apostle Paul did not spend any of his time organising healing shows or concerts, nor chasing the media or gathering money for his ministry. On the contrary, he dedicated his precious time abundantly to local churches, teaching, admonishing and improving the lives of the believers. Five-fold ministers have a great responsibility to prepare the Body of Christ and to train it in order to produce fruit in the Kingdom.

It was never the purpose of each of the five-fold ministries to each build his own ministry, his own name, but only the Body of Christ. The five-fold ministry is directly linked to the local church, because each local church is a field. Television and large stadiums are not fields. The work of the five-fold ministries is not to attract believers to themselves, but to equip them and build them up within the local church.

The next phrase of interest is '*for the edifying of the Body of Christ*', which in Greek is '*eis oikodomin tou somatos tou Xristou*'.

The small preposition before the phrase is especially important in the Greek language. The word '*eis*' suggests an act, a movement in one particular direction – towards the body of Christ and not away from it.

Unfortunately, today we are experiencing the fulfillment of the Apostle Paul's prophecy: '*Also from among yourselves men will rise up, speaking perverse things to draw away the disciples after themselves*' (Acts 20:30, NKJV). It may be that the power and glory that come as a result of being within the five-fold ministry is too big a temptation, and so some have been corrupted.

How many of those who call themselves apostles, prophets, evangelists, pastors or teachers could, if they wanted to, identify with the words of the Apostle Paul in 1 Corinthians 4:13: '*We have been made as the filth of the world, the offscouring of all things until now*' (NKJV).

In English, the phrase, '*till we all come to the unity of the faith*' is mild and implies a well-motivated walk, a path of self-respect in order to reach somewhere. In the Ancient Greek, however, '*mexri katantisomen oi pantes eis tin enotita tis pisteos*' is not at all pleasant. The verb implies a walk that may not be fair and has no consideration of self. In fact, it is a very negative phrase: '*katintisen*' means 'died'; '*mexri katantisomen*' means 'I start on the path heading downwards', 'I become less', 'I am stripped of everything that is mine', 'I leave behind my rights', 'I leave behind my pride, my reputation and my position'. It is a path of removal and denial of self. The Apostle Paul shows us the way to unity on a spiritual map, it is a path of denial of ourselves and abandoning our rights.

The five-fold ministry prepares us, the Church, for this path, teaching us and equipping us to travel it. Unfortunately, today we too often see the 'lone ranger' ministries – autonomous, independent and not accountable to anyone. They take care of themselves without taking the local church into account. There are those who decide whether to visit a church based on how many people are in the congregation and how big the offering is going to be. Once they have finished ministering there and gone on to the next church, they leave behind the seed of an independent spirit. Later, the leadership of the local church has to deal with the fruit of that seed and try to persuade the members that it is not okay to go it alone and that not everybody can become a famous evangelist (or any of the other five-fold ministries). You see, wherever the seed falls, it will bear fruit.

The five-fold ministry should produce dedication to the Lord, humility, obedience and a spirit of service, with the goal of the unity of the Body of Christ. Even if their aim is, theoretically, to invest their life in ministry, when a brother or sister leaves the church it hurts others. The five-fold ministry should leave a simple seed in the Body of Christ: unity through humility, through the removal of rights and titles, through putting the Lord and His Church first and putting themselves last.

> *'From whom the whole body joined and knit together by what every joint supplies, according to the effective working by which every part does its share, causes growth of the body for the edifying of itself in love.'* (Ephesians 4:16. NKJV)

Ephesians 4 is the Apostle Paul describing to us the work and the fruit of the five-fold ministry. This means that whoever introduces himself using one of the titles of the five-fold ministry should be able to show, or at least others should have seen, some of the fruit of his ministry, the way that Paul describes in the above verses.

Let's look at three phrases he included, which are very important and are associated solely with the local church. You cannot talk about '*the whole body joined and knit together by what every joint supplies*' and mean your television audience or the spectators in a stadium.

In the Greek, these phrases are emphatic, with deep meaning and practical application.

The first phrase we'll look at is '*joined*' ('*sinarmologoumenon*'). This Greek word is a compound word, from '*syn*' and '*armologo*'. Its meaning is similar to having to find the use and function of a pile of parts and then connect each to the rest, putting them all in their correct positions to build a machine. It is building with lots of materials which must be combined in a specific way. The five-fold ministry is there to aid and assist in this process. However, this can only be achieved by spending a great amount of time in order to study and get to know each part individually, and ensure that each is taught and guided in a specific direction. This direction must be towards a strong, healthy local church.

Secondly, consider '*knit together*' ('*simvivazomenon*'). This is not a popular word in Greek. '*Simvivazo*' means 'to unite or join', 'to bring to unity', 'to bring closer and create a whole, losing all rights and privileges'. The best picture to help us understand the meaning of the verb is the idea of a choir. A choir is a group of singers with good voices, each well trained and able to sing alone, who have decided to '*simvivastoun*'. They have decided, in other words, to lose a little of their freedom and to come under the rules necessary to function as a group. Each one has a specific job to do. They lose the potential honour of the limelight, glory, reputation and the idea of a glorious solo future in order to create a united, glorious future with their friends. They sacrifice for the body, and that is what the five-fold ministry must produce in the hearts and in the minds of the people of God, not egotistic self-promotion and a demand for personal rights. First and foremost comes the group, the whole, the body.

Finally, '*by what every joint supplies*' ('*dia tis afis tis epihorigias*'). This phrase expresses the strongest element of a healthy five-fold ministry. In the Greek there are two key words: '*afis*', meaning the fifth sense, the sense of touch and '*epihorigias*', meaning support.

The English gives the picture of a body part which gives whatever it can, but this is impersonal and neutral. The Greek expression gives the clear picture of offering and giving support through touching one another, rather than from a distance. Giving support through heart, soul and personal contact are characteristics of a relationship. The Body of Christ is to be united and walk as one in heart-felt relationship.

'*For the love of Christ compels us*' (2 Corinthians 5:14, NKJV). '*Compels us*' ('*sinehi imas*') means that the love of Christ has brought us closer together. Actually, it means that we are so close that we cannot be separated from one another. We are not two separate pieces which are connected, but we are part of one another, we belong to one another. It describes a relationship which is so close, so intense, that my ego is lost. This is the kind of connection that the five-fold ministry should produce.

An apostle cannot enforce laws and rules; giving direction to people he doesn't know. On the contrary, he should come to the local church, stay with the people, get to know them, listen to them, feel their pain, love them, care about them and associate himself with them. He should eat what they eat, sleep as they sleep and stay where they stay. Only then can he, like a father, stand by the people of God and direct them, counsel them, teach them and bear fruit: the fruit of unity, relationship and love.

Acts records the example of the life of the greatest apostle who ever ministered. '*Therefore watch and remember that for three years I did not cease to warn everyone night and day with tears*' (Acts 20:31, NKJV). The field of the five-fold minister is the Church of Christ and especially the local church. The local church is the laboratory where healthy foundations are laid and people are built with godly principles and values, ready to bear fruit to the glory of God. The local church is the potter's workshop.

Let's be careful what seed we allow to fall in our fields, the ground of God. It is time to stop chasing after charismatic personalities, talented people and spiritual signs. We need to chase God and His presence, giving His spirit freedom and license to minister and produce spiritual fruit in our lives and the lives of those in our churches. Christ is building His Church and it is the only thing that He said He will ever build.

Chapter 10

What Do We Learn From the Twelve?

Gordon Tose

The Bible states in 2 Timothy 3:16 that *'All Scripture is God-breathed and is useful'* (NIV). Not some scripture, or most scripture, but *all* scripture. In other words, both the Old Testament and the New Testament are *'useful'*. Each one of the sixty-six books is *'useful'*. What we learn from the lives of Abraham, Joseph, Moses, David and Paul is *'useful'*. Of course, without doubt, the greatest source of wisdom and understanding to be found in the Bible are the words of Jesus Himself. However, a thought that has often crossed my mind is what must it have been like sitting at the feet of Jesus, listening to His words; listening to His wisdom; witnessing first hand His power and His love. Yes, it is wonderful to have the Bible to learn from and build our lives upon, but what an incredible experience to actually be in the physical presence of Jesus. The purpose of this chapter, therefore, is to examine primarily the basic character of those first disciples, and then to see how their characters developed as they walked and talked with Jesus and as they continued their ministry under the power of the Holy Spirit.

The first obvious thing to point out about the disciples is that, on the face of it, they were initially a collection of very ordinary individuals. None of them exercised any real influence in their day-to-day lives. They were, in the main, un-educated and lacking in both wealth and social standing. Yet these were the men Jesus chose: '*You did not choose me, but I chose you and appointed you to go and bear fruit – fruit that will last*' (John 15:16, NIV).

Disciples normally chose the particular rabbi to whom they wanted to be attached, but this was not the case with Jesus' disciples; He chose them, and He did so knowing exactly who and what they were. This is clearly illustrated in the choosing of Nathanael (John 1:43-51). Paul perfectly summarises the kind of people Jesus chooses to use in the following scripture:

> '*Brothers, think of what you were when you were called. Not many of you were wise by human standards; not many were influential; not many were of noble birth. But God chose the foolish things of the world to shame the wise; God chose the weak things of the world to shame the strong. He chose the lowly things of this world and the despised things – and the things that are not – to nullify the things that are, so that no-one may boast before him. It is because of him that you are in Christ Jesus, who has become for us wisdom from God – that is, our righteousness, holiness and redemption. Therefore, as it is written: "Let him who boasts boast in the Lord."*' (1 Corinthians 1:26-31, NIV)

Note that Jesus doesn't have a particular problem with individuals who are intellectually gifted, or influential, or of high social standing. The scripture states that '*not many*' fell into these categories. It does not say that no-one had these attributes.

However, it is interesting that those who were of this kind did seem to find it difficult to give Jesus the pre-eminence He required. For example, the rich young man who sought the assurance of eternal life was unable to elevate Jesus above his material wealth (Matthew 19:16-22). Nicodemus, who was learned, wealthy and influential went to Jesus under the cover of darkness, presumably out of fear of being seen (John 3:1-2). He then found himself in the position of defending Jesus against his fellow Pharisees, yet it was a timid defence (John 7:45-52). His desire to protect was overcome by the risk such a defence would pose to him. Joseph of Arimathea, who was a member of the Sanhedrin (as was Nicodemus) was afraid to publicly acknowlege Christ: '*Now Joseph was a disciple of Jesus, but **secretly** because he feared the Jews*' (John 19:38, NIV).

It would be easy to criticise these three men, but in truth there was much to admire about them. However, what is also true is that what they possessed – their wealth; their social position; their human wisdom – they were unwilling to lay aside to follow Jesus wholeheartedly. Jesus, it seems (who fully understood the frailty of human nature), chose as His first disciples those who would not have to make such a choice.

It is, therefore, a great encouragement to realise that for us to be used by God we do not need to possess any natural ability or find ourselves in advantageous circumstances. In other words, being of use to God is not dependant on what we can bring to Him; it is dependant solely on the faith we have in Him, which leads to a willingness to be used by Him.

Before we look at some of the characteristics of these most ordinary of individuals, it is worth pointing out that the twelve disciples were indeed a diverse group of people; this diversity being highlighted by the choices of Matthew the tax collector and Simon the Zealot.

Most people would regard Matthew as being someone who had 'sold out' his fellow Jews in favour of their Roman masters. Simon, on the other hand, as a Zealot, would look at the Romans with nothing short of hatred. If these two had met anywhere else other than in the presence of Jesus, Simon would no doubt have attempted to kill Matthew.

This union of opposites was not accidental but was in fact a prophetic statement of the Church of the future. The twelve disciples were really a church in miniature; the template for Paul's words to the Colossians: '*Here there is no Greek or Jew, circumcised or uncircumcised, barbarian, Scythian, slave or free, but Christ is all, and is in all*' (Colossians 3:11, NIV).

It would be understandable to assume that the one thing the disciples did have was faith, for '*without faith it is impossible to please God*' (Hebrews 11:6, NIV). This assumption would be correct although, as with Abraham who received three commendations for his faith in that great faith chapter of Hebrews 11, theirs was not a perfect faith. As might be expected, their faith seemed to grow the longer they were with Jesus, but even as their relationship with Him deepened, their lack of faith was still evident at times.

In Matthew 6:25-34 we see that Jesus equates worry with a lack of faith. This principle, which was taught as part of the 'Sermon on the Mount', was obviously something the disciples understood in theory, but not in practice, as can be seen very soon after this teaching when they found themselves on the Sea of Galilee in the middle of a storm. Jesus, who was with them in the boat, was asleep. '*The disciples*', it says, '*went and woke him, saying, "Lord, save us! We're going to drown!" He* (Jesus) *replied,* ***"You of little faith,*** *why are you so afraid?"*' (Matthew 8:25-26, NIV). In Mark 4:40, which records the same incident, Jesus' response is: '*Why are you so afraid?* ***Do you still have no faith?***'. The lesson here for us all is not that Jesus had the power to calm the storm, but that wherever Jesus is, no matter how desperate the situation, nothing should be able to rob us of our peace.

Of course, the more intimate our relationship with Jesus, the easier it is to put this principle into practice, and the disciples had yet to develop their relationship with Him to such a level. Peter was undoubtedly heading in the right direction as, again on the Sea of Galilee, on seeing Jesus walking on the water, he got out of the boat in response to Jesus' instruction to do so. How many steps he took before his faith began to fail him I do not know, but that does not take away from the fact that he did actually walk on the water. In doing so, he proved that his continuing relationship with Jesus was deepening his faith. In fact, at the end of that particular episode, the disciples are inspired to declare: '"*Truly you are the Son of God*"' (Matthew 14:33, NIV).

However, evidence that the development of the disciples' faith was not necessarily in line with what they themselves had experienced is clearly illustrated in Matthew 15, where Jesus, confronted by a crowd in excess of four thousand, instructs the disciples to feed them. '*His disciples answered, "Where could we get enough bread in this remote place to feed such a crowd?"*' (Matthew 15:33, NIV).

On the face of it, this seems an entirely reasonable question until one remembers that in the previous chapter the disciples had not only witnessed Jesus walking on water, but had seen Him feed an even bigger crowd with five loaves of bread and two fish. There was obviously a certain lack of understanding, not so much as to who Jesus was but as to what He could do. Certainly, in the next chapter of Matthew, Jesus links the disciples' lack of faith to their failure to grasp some of the truths He was trying to reveal to them (see Matthew 16:5-12).

Likewise today, a failure to fully understand who Jesus is and what He can do and, out of that, a failure to understand exactly what it is He is instructing us to do, will have the effect of limiting our faith in Him. This, in turn, will limit our effectiveness as Christians. Nevertheless, the disciples' understanding of Jesus was growing:

> '*When Jesus came to the region of Caesarea Philippi, he asked his disciples, "Who do people say the Son of Man is?" They replied, "Some say John the Baptist; others say Elijah; and still others, Jeremiah or one of the prophets." "But what about you?" he asked. "Who do you say I am?" Simon Peter answered, "You are the Christ, the Son of the living God." Jesus replied, "Blessed are you, Simon son of Jonah, for this was not revealed to you by man, but by my Father in heaven."*' (Matthew 16:13-17, NIV)

And as their understanding grew so too did their commitment to Him:

> '*Peter answered him* (on behalf of all the disciples), *"We have left* ***everything*** *to follow you!"*' (Matthew 19:27, NIV)

This was a commitment that led them into dangerous situations:

> '*Then the men stepped forward, seized Jesus and arrested him. With that, one of Jesus' companions* (identified as Peter in John 18:10) *reached for his sword, drew it out and struck the servant of the high priest, cutting off his ear.*' (Matthew 26:50-51, NIV)

It would appear that their faith in Jesus was complete, and yet, in amongst their seemingly unwavering belief in and support of Him, fear and doubt were not entirely done away with.

Who can forget Thomas' words of doubt as the other disciples rejoiced in the resurrection of Jesus? Who can forget – and fail to sympathise with – Peter who, having boasted he would lay down his very life for Jesus, then went on to deny Him; not once, but three times following Jesus' arrest? However, rather than being critical of these lapses of faith, they should actually be an encouragement to us. The reality is that none of us can get it right all the time.

I have already mentioned Abraham as being an example of someone who was full of faith and yet even Abraham, on two occasions, lied about his relationship with his wife because he lacked faith in God to protect him (see Genesis 12:11-13 and Genesis 20:1-2).

The following scripture highlights that God, rather than being ready to punish our lapses of faith, is ever ready to persevere with those whose desire it is to be full of faith, even if their actions are occasionally lacking in faith:

> *'If we are faithless, he will remain faithful, for he cannot disown himself.'* (2 Timothy 2:13, NIV)

There is, however, a note of caution. We cannot assume that our relationship with God will automatically go from strength to strength the longer we know Him. Judas joined Jesus without knowing that he would betray Him. Judas was, therefore, as committed to Jesus as the others – at least outwardly. Unfortunately, for reasons known only to himself, his faith in Jesus diminished to such an extent that he felt justified in his betrayal, until the enormity of what he had done drove him to take his own life. We should all be ever mindful of the words of Paul: *'So, if you think you are standing firm, be careful that you don't fall!'* (1 Corinthians 10:12, NIV). If we think the fate of Judas could never be our fate, then we need to remember that Judas would have thought exactly the same.

The disciples possessed other characteristics less flattering than their evolving faith. In displaying these, they only reinforce my earlier assertion that they were indeed ordinary and much the same as the rest of humanity.

Judgemental

Luke 9:51-56 tells of Jesus' journey to Jerusalem through the region of Samaria. Unfortunately, such was the animosity between Samaritans and Jews that Jesus and His disciples were not welcomed. '*When the disciples James and John saw this, they asked, "Lord, do you want us to call fire down from heaven to destroy them?" But Jesus turned and rebuked them*' (Luke 9:54-55, NIV).

James and John were known as the 'Sons of Thunder' and it is easy to see from this incident why they were known as such. That said, it was still a strange proposal from men who had, for some time now, been in the presence of Jesus. It was especially strange coming from John, who had been with Jesus during the meeting with the Samaritan woman at the well; this meeting having led to many Samaritans believing in Jesus. What this incident clearly shows is the contrast between the harsh spirit of these disciples and the gentle, loving spirit of Jesus.

To understand how Jesus could tolerate this kind of attitude from those He had poured so much of Himself into, it must be remembered that Jesus loves us, not merely for what we are, but also for what we will become. Jesus' faith in John was not misplaced, as John, together with Peter, both having been baptised with the Holy Spirit on the day of Pentecost, emulated Jesus in ministering to the Samaritans (see Acts 8:14-17). *What a difference the Holy Spirit makes in the life of a believer!*

Lacking in compassion

Matthew 15:21-28 tells of the healing of the demon possessed daughter of a Canaanite woman. The mother was obviously in great distress, but that was not the concern of the disciples who viewed her only as a nuisance. '*Send her away*', they insisted, '*for she keeps crying out after us*' (Matthew 15:23, NIV). Compassion is a word much associated with Jesus:

'When he saw the crowds, ***he had compassion on them****, because they were harassed and helpless.'* (Matthew 9:36, NIV)

'When Jesus landed and saw a large crowd, ***he had compassion on them*** *and healed their sick.'* (Matthew 14:14, NIV)

*'Jesus called his disciples to him and said, "****I have compassion for these people.****"'* (Matthew 15:32, NIV)

'Jesus had compassion on them *and touched their eyes. Immediately they received their sight and followed him.'* (Matthew 20:34, NIV)

Part of Jesus' ministry was to heal the sick, and He did so out of compassion. The fact that the woman was a Canaanite gave Jesus some concern, but there was no lack of compassion. The disciples, on the other hand, displayed no such characteristic. Maybe it is harsh to judge them on an isolated incident. Perhaps they were exhausted, although they would be no more exhausted than Jesus; less so in fact, as it was Jesus who had been doing the teaching and performing the ministry.

However, this seems not to have been an isolated incident, as once again mothers brought their children to Jesus only to be met by, what appears to be, the hard hearted disciples (see Matthew 19:13-15). It would appear that compassion was not a strong point of the disciples. What a turn around to read these words of Peter: *'Finally, all of you, live in harmony with one another;* ***be sympathetic****, love as brothers,* ***be compassionate*** *and humble'* (1 Peter 3:8, NIV). It was sympathy and compassion that led Peter and John to heal the crippled beggar at the temple gate (see Acts 3:1-7). *What a difference the Holy Spirit makes in the life of a believer!*

Ambitious

Matthew 20:20-28 tells of James and John's request of Jesus, via their mother, to be given places of honour in the Kingdom of Heaven. This conversation took place only a week or so before Jesus' crucifixion, which meant the disciples had been with Him for almost three years. Despite all this time in the presence of Jesus, selfish ambition was still part of their nature. This particular scripture focuses on James and John, but this character flaw was not limited to these two alone (as can be seen from Mark 9:33-34 and Luke 22:24).

Indeed, ambition – which is the manifestation of pride – is something that can affect each and every one of us. The Bible has some strong words to say about this, linking ambition of this kind to pride, as I have already stated, but also to witchcraft with the devil himself as its source (see Philippians 2:3-4; Galatians 5:19-21 and James 3:13-16). In essence, James and John were asking Jesus to become their tool for advancement. In doing so, they were no guiltier than Christians the world over who treat God like some divine Father Christmas. What a remarkable transformation that these two overly self-seeking individuals should endure the totally selfless acts of martyrdom (in James' case – see Acts 12:2), and exile (in John's case – see Revelation 1:9). *What a difference the Holy Spirit makes in the life of a believer!*

What is interesting is that when the disciples displayed this ambitious side of their nature, it always led to disagreements between them:

> *'Then the mother of Zebedee's sons (James and John) came to Jesus with her sons and, kneeling down, asked a favour of him... When the ten heard about this, they were indignant with the two brothers.'* (Matthew 20:20, 24, NIV)

> *'They came to Capernaum. When he (Jesus) was in the house, he asked them, "What were you arguing about on the road?" But they kept quiet because on the way they had argued about who was the greatest.'* (Mark 9:33-34, NIV)

> *'Also a dispute arose among them as to which of them was considered to be greatest.'* (Luke 22:24, NIV)

What these separate instances highlight is not so much that ambition leads to disagreements, but that disagreements are inevitable during the course of long-term relationships.

This seemingly negative point of view is reinforced by Jesus in His prayer in the Garden of Gethsemane:

> *'My prayer is not for them alone. I pray also for those who will believe in me through their message. (...) May they be brought to complete unity to let the world know that you sent me and have loved them even as you have loved me.'* (John 17:20, 23, NIV)

Here we have Jesus facing crucifixion. John 17 is His final opportunity to really connect with His Father before He goes to the cross. Having prayed for Himself and having prayed for the disciples, Jesus then prayed '*for those who will believe in me*'. In other words, He prayed for us. If we were capable of maintaining relational harmony, then why did Jesus feel the need to pray for us? He prayed for us because He knew that we would find it far easier to fall out with each other than to always be at peace with each other.

What Jesus was saying in His prayer was that the ability to maintain right relationships over the long term is so beyond us, that where true unity exists, it points to God: '*May they be brought to complete* ***unity to let the world know that you sent me and have loved them even as you have loved me***'. In fact God is so aware that this is an area that presents us with a real challenge, that when this challenge is successfully met, He rewards us with His blessing: '*How good and pleasant it is when brothers live together in unity. (...) For there the LORD bestows his blessing*' (Psalm 133:1, 3, NIV).

We can see, therefore, that the disciples were hardly extraordinary. In many ways their characters were representative of the characters of the ordinary, not the extraordinary. Yet despite this, Jesus had great faith in what they would achieve for the Kingdom of God.

> *'Therefore go and make disciples of all nations, baptising them in the name of the Father and of the Son and of the Holy Spirit, and teaching them to obey everything I have commanded you. And surely I am with you always, to the very end of the age.'* (Matthew 28:19-20, NIV)

I believe there were two reasons why Jesus had such confidence in these men. Firstly, they believed. They each believed in who Jesus was with all of their heart. '*You* ***are*** *the Christ, the Son of the living God*' (Matthew 16:16, NIV). I remember when I first became a Christian, and although it was over 27 years ago, the memory of it is as fresh as if it had only been yesterday. I was 32 at the time and was facing a desperate situation. I had no real conviction that God actually existed, but as I cried out to Him, even in my doubt, He wonderfully came into my life and rescued me. However, the thought uppermost in my mind over the following few days was not how much brighter my situation appeared, it was the fact that there was indeed a God.

The disciples never doubted there was a God, but for them to become what was planned for them to become, they first and foremost had to believe in Jesus. If everything they did had not been rooted in their belief in who Jesus was, they would not have fulfilled their destiny. My initial belief in God, which over the years has proved so unshakable, has sustained my faith while the faith of others who have not been as convicted has faltered. Likewise, the faith of the disciples was sustained, often in tremendously difficult circumstances, because of the revelation each of them had concerning Jesus.

However, while belief sustained their faith, something other than belief was needed for them to successfully accomplish what Jesus commanded of them. This second ingredient was the infilling of the Holy Spirit.

> *'But you* (the disciples) *will receive power when the Holy Spirit comes on you; and you will be my witnesses in Jerusalem, and in all Judea and Samaria, and to the ends of the earth.'* (Acts 1:8, NIV)

Being effective witnesses for Christ involves our total lives. It involves what we say and, just as importantly, it involves what we do. Jesus' instruction is to '*let your light shine before men, that they may see your good deeds and praise your Father in heaven*' (Matthew 5:16, NIV). So our witness certainly includes what we do, and yet our deeds by themselves will bring no glory to God unless those who witness them know that God is the motivation behind them.

This makes what we say absolutely vital. Being filled with the Holy Spirit enables us to have a powerful verbal testimony in the form of what we say, which is backed up by a powerful visible testimony in the form of how we live our lives. This visible testimony includes moving in the gifts of the Spirit, but there can be no gifts of the Spirit if there is no infilling of the Spirit. The disciples, having received the

Holy Spirit at Pentecost, were transformed from ineffectual believers into those who spoke with power and who lived in a way which did not nullify the words they spoke.

The Holy Spirit is as relevant today as He was in the days of the disciples. If we want to emulate the power and the effectiveness of those early followers of Jesus, our need of the Holy Spirit is as great as theirs was.

I asked the question: What do we learn from the Twelve? It is my hope that I have demonstrated that it is possible for every Christian to be as useful to God as the disciples were. This is because, far from being spiritual 'supermen', they displayed all the frailties and weaknesses that beset every single one of us. However, as surely as they rose to the challenge, so too can we all.

Chapter 11
Characteristics of a Father
Colin Cooper

What a great day we live in, what a time to be alive! The Lord is restoring truth back into His Church with an ever-increasing momentum.

In this great day we hear much about fathers, based on the scripture 1 Corinthians 4:15 which says that there are many guardians in Christ but not many fathers; or many teachers but not many fathers.

My father died when I was seven. I remember him very clearly and I loved him and believed he loved me. I didn't have the benefit of that love for long, but they are good memories. We had a small yacht that we would go sailing on for days on end and I loved being with him. He was a loving father. Many years later, as a teenager, I found out that he was not my real father, but I had been fostered by the couple I called my mother and father.

The fathering security was absent in my teenage years so I had no father to instruct me, which led me to do some foolish things. Once I was in jail for hurting someone in a fight, I was punished by the system for what was classed as causing grievous bodily harm to another person.

Sometime later, a young man called John McKale stopped me on a street and told me about a person called Jesus. The following week

I went with him to a church in the city of Newcastle-Upon-Tyne which was called Bethshan Tabernacle. There I found a man called Herbert Harrison who gave guidance from the platform as to how I should live. Although relationships were not understood in the mid '60s, I still looked to Herbert as a father, which looking back brought some security into my life.

Today's sociologists tell us that children of single parent families, where there is no father present, do less well at school and may not be as secure in life. This by no means is meant to frown upon single mothers, who do an amazing job with their children, but it is just a fact of life that without a father in their lives children don't achieve as much.

As in the natural, so it is in the spiritual. This helps us understand the spiritual.

Today, there are many spiritual orphans who have never been fathered, who in turn are not sure how to father. This then has an effect on relationships in the church, and without real relationships nothing works long term. *Everything* comes out of relationships.

Like a natural family with mothers, fathers, brothers and sisters, so is the spiritual family. We have mothers in the Lord, fathers, brothers and sisters. A father in the Lord understands he is part of an amazing supernatural family.

- Ephesians 3:14-15 talks about family in heaven and on earth.
- Psalm 68:5 says that God is a Father to the fatherless.
- Isaiah 64:8 says that the Lord is our Father.

How does this reflect on an earthly father?

1 Corinthians 15:49 says that we bear the likeness of the man from heaven.

Wow, what a statement! A father on this earth, whether named as an apostle or some other gifting, will reflect the likeness of the Lord. So this is why we call them fathers or mothers in the Lord. What an amazing earthy family we are in:

- Jesus is our elder brother (Hebrews 2:14-17).
- Jesus, the elder brother, is over God's house (Hebrews 3:6).
- Jesus was the first born among the brothers (Romans 8:29).
- We follow the example of our elder brother who has been through the problems that we go through (1 Peter 2:21).
- Kids are born into this family (John 1:12-13).
- We are partakers of the same blood (John 6:53).
- The family on earth derives its name from the Father (Ephesians 3:15).
- We bear His likeness, so we have a family resemblance (1 Corinthians 15:49).
- We are born into this family with a seed that has no blight (1 Peter 1:23).
- God will put lonely people into families (Psalm 68:6).

Families have a father

Today, I hear some men claim to be apostles but they have never built a church in their lives, so they have no spiritual family. An apostle will be a father with kids all around him.

A father mentors his sons

Jesus mentored His disciples (Luke 6:12-16; Mark 3:13-19). Jesus wanted His kids with Him (Acts 4:13). People knew that the disciples had been with Jesus.

The fathers pass on an inheritance. Moses passed on his spiritual genes to Joshua, Paul passed his genes to Timothy. Paul said in 2 Timothy 1:2, '*Timothy, my dear son*' – this was more than a working relationship. Paul had a fatherly, loving heart towards Timothy.

Paul mentored Timothy (Acts 16:1-4; 2 Timothy 1:1-7; 2 Timothy 3:14-17). Paul took Timothy:

- With him to establish churches.
- With him in Philippi and in the house of Lydia where all were saved.
- With him in Philippi when he was imprisoned.
- With him in Thessalonica.
- With him in Berea.

- With him in Athens on Mars Hill.
- With him in Antioch (read Acts 16-20 – Paul's two journeys).

A father will challenge and comfort us with the Word of God

1 Thessalonians 2:11-12 says, '*For you know that we dealt with each of you as a father deals with his own children, encouraging, comforting and urging you to live lives worthy of God, who calls you into his kingdom and glory*'.

I remember as a very young boy, my foster father correcting me on something and I thought he was the most evil person in the world. Of course he was not, but my carnal, sinful nature did not want correction. The Bible tells us to honour fathers and mothers in the Lord (Ephesians 6:2-3), then things will be well with us. When we forget to honour, that relationship with a father can be easily broken. In these days of broken relationships, don't walk away from your father because of correction or because you think he has some weaknesses.

Fathers have sons. Elijah had Elisha, Paul had Timothy and Moses had Joshua. An apostle today should have sons. Sons are different from a group of men employed by someone called an apostle. Often we hear apostles talk about teams who are with them, but in reality they are an employed committee.

A great example of a fathering heart is seen in Acts 15:37-39. Barnabas wanted to take John Mark with them on a ministry trip, but Paul had little faith in John Mark because he had deserted them in Pamphylia and had left the work they were doing. So Paul had little patience with John Mark.

Barnabas had great patience with John Mark and saw the potential in him. He fathered him and developed his character. A father can see the potential in a son, and father someone even if they have failed in the past.

Paul had fathered sons but it is interesting that he did not do this with John Mark. When true apostles work, they are not superstars. They have no problems working with others of similar gifting. So when a father does not relate to a person, there is someone else on the team who that person can relate to and so they do not have to leave the church. But as time goes by they will begin to relate with the rest of the team through the ministry of the father.

A father works for a future generation

A father does not try to build an image for himself and Ecclesiastes 2:18-21 sums it up. All his labours will be given to someone else, but will he squander what has been given or will he be a son and increase the work?

Fathers bring a feeling of security because there is an understanding that they are working for the good of others.

A father prepares people

Principles of preparation:

- The Israelites were prepared by the father to pass over Jordan (Joshua 1:11).
- Samuel prepared men's hearts (1 Samuel 7:3).
- Paul was prepared over 13 years.
- Moses was prepared over 14 years.
- Joseph was prepared over 13 years.
- Joshua was prepared over 14 years.
- Jesus was prepared over 30 years.

A father is someone who has been tried and tested. They must first be tested, or tried and proven (1 Timothy 3:10).

The Church needs those who have gone through the fires and pressures and have been formed into godly characters.

Chapter 12

From Pastor to Apostle

Some Thoughts on the Apostolic Ministry

Dick Iverson

I had the privilege of being an evangelist in my earlier days and was tutored under T.L. Osborn. I held crusades with my wife in a number of different countries, and I thank God for the evangelistic experience I had preaching to great crowds of people. I realised in that season of time that it was my calling, although I always felt in my heart that I would pastor some day.

After ten years as an evangelist, I took over as senior pastor from my dad at our church in Portland. I had actually labored with him as a co-pastor from the very beginning, in 1951, but I was in-and-out a lot, ministering in different countries. The adjustment from being an evangelist to being a pastor was very difficult. As an evangelist I was always on the move. I had a number of messages that would inspire faith and bring people to Christ, and then I would pray for the sick. We would draw large crowds with this ministry, but I would generally only stay two or three weeks in one area and then move on.

When you become a pastor you are there all 52 weeks of the year and your dozen-or-so messages don't last very long; the people want something fresh and new. This became quite a challenge once I ran out of my best messages! Now I had to really go to the Word and develop a deeper line of ministry.

As a pastor, I loved to go through books of the Bible and do character studies or topical themes. I would stay on them for maybe five or six weeks before I would move on. Every year I did my best to cover the topics of prayer, worship, evangelism, stewardship, giving, missions and so on, weaving them into my messages from different angles. I realised I needed to 'make the basics beautiful' and I felt that I was feeding the people correctly.

The church began to grow and young people were coming who wanted to be trained for the ministry. In 1967 we started Portland Bible College. Bible Temple became a fathering church as we launched a number of church plants throughout the United States and even internationally.

I realised that my role was slowly changing from that of a pastor to an apostolic covering for churches.

I remember a 19 year old Portland Bible College student, who recognised me as an apostle, coming to me one day. He told me that God had called him to be an apostle and that he would like me to train him to become one. I told him that I would be happy to do so but first he had an assignment that was essential. I asked him to go out and pastor a church for 20 years. Then, if he was successful at pastoring a church, I would consider working with him in his apostolic calling. Needless to say, he walked away with a saddened heart because he expected to be an apostle at 19 years of age.

Apostles are gifts whom God has given to the Church. It is not something you personally choose to be. The call to the ministry of an apostle begins with the Lord putting a certain desire in your heart to want to work with other pastors. Not all pastors will become apostles and not all apostles will be pastors first. But there is something about pastoring a church and pastoring leaders in the church that naturally develops apostolic ministry.

It is a lot like being an apprentice carpenter. The apprentice hangs around and just picks up the lumber for awhile. Pretty soon he pounds a few nails, and then he learns to do a little more, and after a time he can build a house. You could call him a 'carpenter' at the beginning, but he really wasn't. That was his long-term destiny.

I've met pastors in their thirties who are apostolic in nature. By that I mean they are always thinking about other pastors, how they can help them through difficult times. They may not have any official connection with that church, they just have a heart for serving and helping. Over time their apostolic calling will emerge.

Just because you pastor a large church doesn't mean that you will transition into apostolic ministry. Many pastors of large churches are concerned only for their church. I don't think they have an apostolic calling until they have a larger circle of burden and vision. Not only do apostles have a heart for their own church, they also have a heart for other churches. In other words, an apostle should be the kind of person who sows in another man's field and not just his own.

A person is recognised as an apostle because he has real relationships with people he is 'apostling' and not just because he has some kind of word that he is an apostle. You must earn that level of respect, not demand it. Respect and trust are earned over time. If you haven't proven over a period of years that you love people and are there to serve them, they won't follow your 'fatherly' advice just because you showed up.

I believe that apostolic authority functions voluntarily. Apostles must understand their authority. Some people teach that the apostle is 'the' authority. He's worked his way to the top and now he has ultimate authority over certain churches. That's very dangerous. That's not the way Paul operated. If anybody should have, he should, but he reminded the church at Corinth that he did not have dominion over their faith and that he was just a '*helper of their joy*' (2 Corinthians 1:24). One translation says '*partner of your joy*'. I feel that is the spirit of an apostle: 'I'm not taking dominion over your life, I am a helper'.

Some people see apostles as being so dominant that when they walk into a church, the resident eldership just sits down and makes all the course adjustments the apostle requires of them. Then when the apostle leaves he hands the reins of the church back to the leadership. That's not only unbiblical, it is very dangerous. Everything in God's Kingdom is to do with relationships. So whenever you try to define an apostolic relationship in terms of hierarchy, things break down very quickly.

I often look at the apostolic role as that of a grandfather. You can't really be a grandfather unless you had children that you raised successfully, and then they had children. As a grandfather, you then have influence over the lives of the grandchildren. I think, as the scripture says, first the natural and then the spiritual (1 Corinthians 15:46), that this concept is right.

If I walked into my married son's home, with his children, and I saw something out of order, I would not say anything to the children but would go to my son and say, 'I don't think you should do this or that to your children.' I know he can say 'Dad, that's the way we're going to raise our children' and my authority would be over. Even if I was right, he is responsible for his own children.

Hebrews 13 says of the oversight of the church that we are to obey those who have the rule over us, for they must give an account for our souls. As an apostle, I don't have to give an account for the congregation. My responsibility ends after speaking into the lives of my married spiritual sons and daughters. I owe it to them to be gracious, but to speak the truth in love.

As stated earlier, everything is built on relationships. I have found over the years that relationships change over time. In the case of a new church plant, I make more of an effort to speak into that church in its embryo state. But then as the church grows, the nature of our relationship changes.

It's kind of like raising a child. A day will come when your child is a young adult and looks you straight in the eye and you realise that he knows as much about some things as you do. You'll still have his respect, but he doesn't need you now in the same way he did when he was a baby. He has grown, he has matured, and so your relationship must move to a more equal basis.

That's not a threat to me personally. I'm thrilled when I walk into a church that was once fragile and struggling for survival and is now a powerful, strong church. That church does not need me in the same way they may have earlier. We will always be friends and I will always be there for them, but I now have the opportunity to give some of my time elsewhere.

I have tried to avoid what I have watched happen with some of my friends who never let their sons grow up. They kept the lid on the decision process. They felt they should tell their sons what to teach and preach, how to act, and what to do and not to do. That may be acceptable when you're little and you're trying to learn how to walk. But once a son has his own children then it is abnormal for someone to come in and tell them how to raise their family.

My approach is to be more hands-on when they are young and could hurt themselves unnecessarily, but as soon as I can, to back off and give them room to be themselves and develop their own personalities. My 'sons' all have different ministry styles and their churches all function with their own emphases, but they are all great men of God. They may lead differently from the way I might lead, but I can't fault them. They all have their own personalities. What is important is that we share our common church principles and core distinctives.

So the bottom line is this: moving from the role of a pastor to that of an apostle really takes time. Again, first the natural and then the spiritual. You have to prove your apostolic right by being successful in seeing your own children grow up as a godly seed. How can you tell someone how to raise their children if you have not been successful in raising your own? And, I might add, apostolic ministry is actually apostolic *work*!